Wind in the Wires

DUNCAN GRINNELL-MILNE

Wind in the Wires

And there was somewhere in me the thought:
'By Jove! this is the deuce of an adventure—
something you read about'
> Joseph Conrad, *Youth*

 JARROLDS, LONDON

JARROLDS PUBLISHERS (LONDON) LTD
3 Fitzroy Square, London W1

AN IMPRINT OF THE HUTCHINSON GROUP

London Melbourne Sydney Auckland
Wellington Johannesburg Cape Town
and agencies throughout the world

First published 1933
This revised and reset edition 1971

This book has been set in Times type, printed in Great Britain
on antique wove paper by Anchor Press, and
bound by Wm. Brendon, both of Tiptree, Essex

ISBN 0 09 107800 8

Contents

Illustrations

Principal Officers Identified from Nicknames

16 SQUADRON

The Starched Shirt—Major H. C. T. (Stuffy) Dowding, RA (later Air Chief Marshal Lord Dowding, RAF)

Growl—Captain C. Wigram, RFC

Wilhelm or Little Willie—Lieutenant H. S. Ward, RFC

Dante—(Observer) Captain C. Strong, TA

56 SQUADRON

Gilly—Major E. J. L. W. Gilchrist, 9th Lancers and RFC, O.C. 56 Squadron

Shutters—Lieutenant R. F. Shutes, RFC and RAF

Johnny—Captain John Speaks, RFC and RAF (American)

Larry—Lieutenant Laurence G. Bowen, RFC and RAF (American). Killed in action, 15 September 1918

The Newt—Lieutenant D. S. C. Newton, RAF

The acting-adjutant—Lieutenant W. E. Clarkson, RAF

Author's Note

It is, in my view, a singularly happy circumstance that this new edition should be brought out by Jarrolds since they belong to the same publishing group, Hutchinson, as do Hurst & Blackett who published the original. Thus, after numerous appearances in print, not all of them free from error, in Britain and the United States, the full publishing circle has been described and the book, once more between hard covers, is back where it started from many years ago.

Another circumstance did not, at first, strike me as nearly so happy. In fact the idea put forward by an enthusiastic publisher's reader that, to make the new edition genuinely new, I should carry out comprehensive cover-to-cover modifications filled me with such alarm that I came near to rejecting the project out of hand. I had already, for an earlier edition, made fairly extensive amendments; to embody the vast changes now suggested would, as I saw it, be tantamount to throwing the whole book away and writing another. Short of that, I could see no sure way of improving upon the most recent version.

It was therefore with little hope of success that I began the task of revision. Almost at once, however, re-reading my own words after a long interval, I was reminded of Wilde's judgement that, in time, 'all work criticises itself'—a painful truth in whose profundity I perceived my exceptional good fortune. For it must of necessity be somewhat rare for both an author and his work to survive for the better part of forty years, and for the author then to be given the opportunity to amend words and passages where the work has come to

'criticise itself'. Understanding of this made revision so much
more acceptable that, in the end, there was scarcely a page
of the corrected version that did not show signs of those
amendments which time and mature reflection had forced
upon me.

At this point I must hasten to reassure the various readers
who, faithful to the original, have written to express anxiety
at the rumoured news that the book was to be radically
altered for the new edition. To them I would say that, whilst
the numerous amendments scattered throughout the text
ensure that this is indeed a new edition, the book as a whole
remains unchanged. A couple of short passages, judged to
be out of place here, have been deleted, a few redundant
sentences cut, some unnecessary adjectives removed, certain
character sketches made more concise. One section has been
re-written, that dealing with the years of captivity, where I
have slightly expanded the 'escaping' adventures, not
because they are directly connected with flying—save in the
lowlier sense of fleeing!—but because they have a certain
relevance to my subsequent adventures in France. Elsewhere,
I have retained a number of pages first inserted in the
Mayflower paperback of 1966. These pages constitute, as I
wrote in the preface to that edition, 'an account of something
that, at the very end of the war, made a lasting impression
upon me. The account, omitted (for lack of space) from the
first and succeeding editions, eventually found its way into
a collection of short stories. I have now restored it to the
place where it properly belongs.' Persistent readers of the
book who have been kind enough to advise me are unani-
mous in declaring that the restoration is justified.

Mention of those helpful readers leads me to single out
one of many: my good friend Alex Revell, whose knowledge
of all things concerning the Royal Flying Corps never ceases
to astonish me. More than supply sound advice—at my own
urgent request—about what might be revised and, still
further, what must be allowed to stand in the new edition,
he has been instrumental in supplying illustrations from
hitherto unpublished photographs. Of these I feel bound, if
only for personal reasons, to give pride of place to the one
listed as 'Remains of 4086'. Its significance and the manner
in which it was traced deserve to be explained here.

Appropriate photographs from the early days of war-flying are not always easy to come by and Revell, in the course of his search, had occasion to consult Alex Imrie, whose collection of more than 12,000 items, mostly from German sources, must surely be unique. From the majority of these photographs Imrie's patient research has enabled him to identify men and machines, German as well as British, together with places and dates; but there was one, showing a charred fuselage, that had eluded research. Distinguishable upon the tail-fin, however, was a serial number and this Revell showed to J. M. Bruce, the foremost expert on British aircraft of World War I. After careful study of his records Bruce was able to announce that '4086' was the number of a B.E.2c belonging to 16 Squadron in 1915 and reported missing early in December of that year. Since only one machine had been lost by the squadron that month, he had no hesitation in stating that Imrie's photograph was of the selfsame machine that had carried me into captivity.

This struck me as so startling a conclusion that, although both Revell and Imrie supported Bruce, I found it very hard to believe. I had no recollection whatever of any serial number, yet despite the experts' opinion I had some reason for thinking it could not be 4086. The one remaining hope of verification lay in my Pilot's Log Book, a scrappy affair abominably written, for the most part in pencil, and containing, to my shame, hardly any details of interest or importance; I doubt whether I have consulted it more than twice in forty years . . . Now, opening it by chance at the right page, the scrawled evidence lay instantly before my eyes. From October, through November, up to and including the fateful first of December 1915, I had flown but one aircraft: 'B.E.2c. Number 4086'.

With all doubts resolved I studied that astonishing photograph more closely. There it lies, the fuselage with its charred longerons—all, I suppose, that was worth the salvaging, for the observer's seat and centre-section went up in the holocaust of my contriving and the engine was wrecked before ever we landed. There is the pilot's seat, scorched by the flames our old enemy the West Wind so helpfully blew back, the seat that had carried me for long hours and through many an adventure, from which a few minutes earlier I had climbed hastily, and for the last time, leaving the safety-belt hanging over the side. That one small detail is, to me, the most impressive of all; it brings in a flash and into the immediate present an event from which I am now separated by the unbelievable distance of fifty-five years; and my enduring astonishment at the sudden reality of an old photograph is a measure of the debt of gratitude owed to those who traced and identified the truncated remains of 4086.

To the same enthusiastic experts, Revell and Imrie, I am also indebted for some half a dozen other photographs of men and machines of the period; and, when so much else has been mislaid or irretrievably 'borrowed', I am fortunate indeed to have been able to supply two or three of my own. More would, I think, have been too many; because I must stress, for the benefit of new readers, that this is not a book of technical information concerning aeroplanes, arms and equipment; nor does it contain lists of gallant pilots, their countless fights and numerous 'victories'. To describe what it is, I cannot do better than quote the last paragraph of the earlier preface. There, after citing Conrad's *Youth*— quoted here upon the title-page—I went on to say that this was the book's sole purpose: to tell a tale of personal adventure sometimes joyful, occasionally miserable where, as in all warfare, long days of boredom are punctuated by moments of anxiety so intense that, at the time, I could have wished myself safe in bed and a thousand miles away. There is no discussion of causes or strategy. No discordant noises of the sort made nowadays by bickering historians or frustrated politicians can be heard above the wild music that sang through the wires of our primitive aircraft. What is remembered is uncomplicated: the haunting thrill of the early days of flying, the beauty of perilous skies above Artois and Picardy, the nicknames of old friends, and some small part of the fortunes of two valiant squadrons of the old Royal Flying Corps—Number 16 and the ever-glorious Number 56. With them in mind the original dedication stands. Despite the passing of the years it is still fitting.

> *To those who flew*
> *To those who fought*
> *To those who fell*

Part One

1

The Wings Start to Grow

In July, 1915, I left the infantry regiment to which I belonged to be attached to the Royal Flying Corps. The meaning behind the word 'attached' was that the employment should be purely conditional. Like a defendant in a breach of promise case, I might claim to be attached but not definitely engaged. My status remained that of an infantry officer; if I were found to be unsuitable as a pilot, or if once in the air I discovered an unconquerable dislike for aviation, then I could return without let or hindrance to my battalion. There was no binding engagement to metamorphose me into an airman or, failing that, to use me in any capacity at all in the flying branch of the Army. It so happened, however, that my temporary posting became permanent and lasted for more than a dozen years of war and peace. This is, in part, the record of the first four of those years.

I

I arrived at Shoreham-on-Sea after dark. On the way from London, or rather during the change of trains at Brighton, I met an officer bound for the same destination. His name was on his luggage-labels, together with the address of the particular Reserve Air Squadron which I myself was to join. As he was a subaltern and as I saw no signs of his being a qualified aviator, I was not more than usually awed by the fact that he was a gunner. I had hoped that in aviation he would be as much of a novice as I was, but in the course of conversation he informed me that he had been at Shoreham quite a long time, that he was in fact just returning from leave which, I knew, was not usually granted until one had fully qualified. My respect for him increased.

I asked him about the squadron. He was very willing to talk and the first impression he gave me was encouraging: few parades, no unnecessary drill, no compulsory church on Sundays, rather more liberty than in an infantry regiment— provided, of course, that one 'got on well'. That, to me, meant showing promise as a pilot; my head was, so to speak, already in the air. And my companion must, I thought, be something of an expert, spending most of each day off the ground, for he told me that he 'simply loved the work'.

But a little later he let fall that he was struggling to qualify as a squadron adjutant and had practically given up the idea of becoming an active service pilot. Also he told me that no one did much flying at Shoreham and that after a few days' trial many officers returned to their regiments. I was not quite so sure that I was going to 'love the work'.

At Shoreham station a Crossley tender* met us—that, at any rate, was a step up from the infantry!—and took us over to the Mess in a bungalow near the sea. There, in addition to an air of comfortable informality, I found cheese, biscuits and beer.

II

The next day was Saturday, no parades but attendance at the aerodrome. From the mess to the aerodrome was perhaps as much as a mile; we were driven there in a Crossley tender.

In the sheds was a collection of aircraft, most of them interesting museum pieces in which we were to be instructed, and two dangerous-looking single-seaters (said to be capable of ninety miles an hour!) with which, I was glad to hear, we were to have no dealings whatsoever. There were about half a dozen of us novices and the same number of older pupils.

* Crossley Motors supplied all the RFC's transport from 'workshop lorries' to the squadron 'touring car'. The 'tender' was a light personnel-carrier.

The instructors were pre-war regular officers, of the rank of Captain; they had flown in France, had actually been fired at in the air, had survived engine failures, forced landings, rifle fire and thunderstorms. We regarded them as living evidence that the Age of Heroes had come again.

During the morning one of the museum pieces was wheeled from its shed and set down upon the edge of the turf. With much pushing and pulling it was carefully arranged so as to face the wind, although to us laymen the manœuvre was a little obscure, since the bows of the aeroplane were almost identical with its stern. It had an elevator—or stabilising surface—stuck out in front upon curving outriggers of wood, and a double set of stabilisers—or elevators— fixed to wooden spars at the stern. But for the propeller which drove the machine inexorably forward and the arrangement of the pilot's seat and controls, it might have been designed to travel in either direction. Officially it was called after its inventor: a Maurice Farman biplane; but it was better known as a 'Longhorn', because of the outriggers to the forward elevator. A slightly more modern sister-ship was called the 'Shorthorn', because the inventor had, rather rashly we thought, done away with the outriggers and elevator; and taking them all round the *vaches mécaniques* of Monsieur Farman's breeding were pleasant beasts. But except for slowness and docility the resemblance to cows ended with the horns. To the uninitiated eye the Longhorn presented a forest of struts and spars, with floppy white fabric drooped over all, and enough piano wire to provide an impenetrable entanglement. At the sight of the craft before us, we put our heads on one side like puzzled terriers.

Presently the Longhorn's engine was started up. It was a Renault of uncertain strength, eight-cylindered, air-cooled, small but wonderfully reliable. When running slowly it made a noise suggesting a pair of alarm-clocks ticking upon a marble mantelpiece.

One of the instructors and a senior pupil picked their way through the wire entanglements, stepped over the wooden horns where they curved to the ground to become skids, mounted upon the wheels and clambered with a good deal of difficulty into the *nacelle*. No, it was not a body, nor a fuselage, nor yet a cockpit; it was a *nacelle*. The same name is used for the baskets that hang beneath balloons, but this *nacelle* was not of wicker. It was smooth and fairly solid-looking. It recalled the bath in which Marat was murdered. Doubtless to remove this ominous impression it had been painted a nice cheerful blue. . . . The pilot and his passenger settled down into their elevated seats, adjusted goggles, helmets, and took a long look round as though it might be their last. After listening awhile to the engine, the pilot waved hands, attendant mechanics removed wooden blocks from beneath the wheels, and the machine moved forward slowly, lurching slightly over the uneven ground like a cow going out to pasture. The alarm-clocks ticked much louder; the forest of struts, the network of piano-wire, the *nacelle* with its occupants, all hanging rather mysteriously together, moved away at increasing speed. The draught from the propeller rippled the grass, rushing back to make us duck and clutch at our caps.

When I looked again the Longhorn was scurrying across the aerodrome at the most alarming speed. It seemed incredible that the various parts should still be holding together. The machine hugged the ground; the curving horns, the wheels and skids, the tail-booms were all buried in the uncut grass through which the propeller seemed to be blazing a trail, and that and the noise of the receding engine made me think of nothing so much as a lawnmower running amok. I watched, holding my breath. And—lo!—it began to unstick from the earth. It rose a few inches; higher; it flew! O wondrous contrivance: 'Hail to thee, blithe spirit, bird thou never wert!' Shelley should have been a pilot.

III

Nowadays such a machine in flight would seem ridiculous even to a child; but to us it was impressive enough. It was flying: that alone was sufficient. There in the sky was an aeroplane in which we could take a personal interest, in which presently we too would ascend, not as passengers but as pupils. It was very thrilling.

We watched that antiquated cage of a machine as if it were our own property. We noted the manner of its leaving the ground, followed its course in the distance, observed how it banked at the turns, held our breath as it glided in to land as gently as any thistledown. We forbore from criticism, we did not even remark to each other how, flying into the wind, this Longhorn appeared to have solved the problem of hovering like a helicopter, so low against the breeze was its forward speed. Nor did we discuss the value of such a craft in war. No matter what its limitations, this machine was to give up to us its one priceless secret, the mystery of how to fly. With luck we might some day progress to swifter, more deadly aircraft, but in this one we would first learn to grow our wings. She (*it* for such a venerable machine is not nearly enough)—she would foster the fledgelings. And out of a hundred craft, her we should never forget. . . .

We crowded round when she came to rest in front of the sheds. The instructor got down from the *nacelle*, gave orders for the machine to be put away and strode forward with an expressionless face. A pupil braver than the rest of us made so bold as to ask: 'Will there be any flying today? Instructional flying?'

The instructor chewed a piece of grass.

'No,' he said curtly, 'it's not good enough.'

There was a wisp of cloud at about a thousand feet from the ground; the wind speed was perhaps as much as ten miles an hour. Out to sea it was a little misty. No, it was clearly not good enough.

'You didn't get very high during your flight,' another pupil remarked to the lucky one who had been passenger, a grave individual who seldom spoke to the novices because he had been a motor salesman before the war and had then taken a few lessons in piloting which placed him upon a higher level than the rest of us. He pushed his way through our crowd, looking rather grim and haughty.

'Of course we didn't get high!' he answered, and there was a rebuke in his tone. 'We could hardly get off the ground. No lift in the air.'

He seemed very wise as I watched him stroll away. Here, thought I, was another complexity added to the puzzling business of aviation. One had to study the air. The wind must be of a certain strength, the clouds at a given height and of known density. In addition there was something of which I as yet knew nothing. I must learn to sniff the air like an old hound, a flying hound; to judge the quality of the atmosphere from the wind upon my cheeks; to feel its nature between finger and thumb. Otherwise I might some day embark upon a flight only to find that there was 'no lift in the air'—whatever that might mean.

IV

'In aviation,' a friend of mine was wont to say, 'there is as much art as science.' And there is more in this remark than is at first apparent. Pursuits there are and professions that demand science and nothing else; for instance one may suppose that putting a man on the moon calls for a great deal of science but for very little art. On the other hand certain arts have scant need of science to bring them to fruition. A poet is not necessarily a scientist, not even as much of a chemist as Keats; and with aeronautics, in its earlier stages, art often seemed to be marching ahead of a science that was in its infancy and waiting for the pilots whose progressive discoveries, be it said, were frequently the result of accident.

I began to glean information concerning my new calling.

To be successful, I gathered, a pilot must learn to steer a steady course between the Charybdis of 'spinning', the remedy for which was not yet known, and the Scylla of diving into the hard, hard ground. 'Stalling'—that was a word I heard on everyone's lips: to lose flying-speed and, in consequence, all control of the machine. There were other minor difficulties to be reckoned with, mainly those connected with the strength—or rather the weakness—of the aeroplanes of those days. At all points one encountered either the unknown, or the more or less certain structural dangers. It was, they told me, courting death to dive the majority of machines at any appreciable angle, the speed and increased strain would pull the wings off. To bank too steeply might involve a sideslip or loss of flying-speed, either of which might quickly develop into the irremediable spin. 'Looping' had, of course, been done and overdone before the war, but only on machines strong enough to stand the strain.

Had anyone attempted to loop a Longhorn, the poor thing would have tied herself into knots. And since looping was of no value by itself it was neither taught nor encouraged on any type of machine.

Before coming to Shoreham I had been taken up as a passenger several times, so that I had a rudimentary knowledge of flying. But now I perceived what innumerable lessons there were to be learned, anxiously, attentively, before one could hope to become an artist worthy of the name of Air Pilot. The whole business was unpleasantly suggestive of tight-rope walking, the margins of safety were so narrow. A Longhorn—and a good many other machines for that matter—would leave the ground at well under forty miles an hour, and I doubt if her top speed ever exceeded forty-six or seven whatever may have been calculated on paper. This gave one a variation of some ten miles an hour; if you went too fast something fell off or snapped; if any slower you stalled, spun, dived, slipped one way or another and ended for a certainty by breaking your neck. And then there was the question of the engine. At full power it was just enough to get one safely off the ground and to climb high enough for turning, but if you ran it at too great a speed the engine would overheat, and at the slightest loss of power the nose of the machine had to be pushed well down to maintain flying-speed. A tricky business!

In the Mess we talked a great deal of shop.

V

Eighteen is an impressionable age, especially for a budding pilot, so that it is not surprising that the first real lessons—roughly, horribly taught—should have been driven into me with such force that I never afterwards forgot them. It happened on a Sunday, the very first Sunday at Shoreham.

The day of the week did not make much difference to the routine of a Flying Corps squadron. If it were fine and there were machines available and pupils to be taught, instruction took place as usual, save that early flying was cancelled, we got up later and spent more time over breakfast. A stiff breeze came off the sea and the large masses of damp cloud everywhere would have made it far too bumpy for Long-horn work. But we strolled down to the sheds because we were all young enough to enjoy stroking our cows in the byre, even if we could not have them brought out for exercise.

At the aerodrome a treat was in store for us. A brand-new aeroplane of the most modern type had just arrived on a visit. It was being flown around the country upon a series of test flights by a well-known pilot from the Royal Aircraft Factory at Farnborough, accompanied by a civilian expert. We gathered about it in silent wonder, mindful of the pilot's request that we should not touch anything.

It was sheer joy to examine such a machine at close quarters. Those of us who had flown as passengers before coming to Shoreham had seen a good many sorts of ancient aircraft; all the greater now was our interest and admiration. The engine of this biplane was in front (like some German machines I had seen before the war), whereas most of those we knew by sight had it astern—'pushers'—and the body was long, narrow, neatly shaped. The wings were thicker than those of Maurice Farman machines; they looked solid, strong. The bracing wires were no longer cable or piano, they were of a new design: 'streamline'. In the pilot's cockpit was a neat dashboard with instruments. The controls were operated by a straight 'stick', not 'handlebars' as in the Longhorn; there was a rudder bar instead of pedals. The tanks were said to contain fuel for more than four hours' flying and it was evident that in addition to the passenger this aeroplane would be capable of carrying a machine-gun or bombs. An improvement upon older models of the same type, it was believed to attain no less than seventy-six miles an hour at full speed. It was known as the B.E.2c.; its engine was the 90 horse-power 'R.A.F.' —the letters standing for Royal Aircraft Factory, the home of those expert minds whose latest conception now stood before us.

I gazed at the pilot with envy while imagination soared faster than the swiftest biplane. Some day I too would wear Flying Corps 'Wings' upon the left breast of my tunic, I too would steer a wonderful B.E.2c. and learn to manœuvre it with graceful ease. I would fly such a machine in France; my wings would darken the skies above the expectant battlefront, the enemy's secrets would be disclosed to me.

At my approach Zeppelins would hurry home, their huge sheds leap up in flames beneath my deadly rain of bombs, Berlin would pass sleepless nights. And at the end I would make a perfect landing before the assembled heads of the Flying Corps. . . .

At lunch in the mess that day we were very quiet, listening in awed silence to the instructors and the pilot from Farnborough discussing technicalities almost entirely over our heads. It was thrilling to hear the names of famous airmen bandied familiarly about, to hear of all the different types of aeroplanes with exaggerated speeds which we might hope to fly, and particularly to hear this so experienced pilot (a test pilot!) give his views on how to do this and that, how to turn quickly and with almost vertical banking, how to do a spiral glide, how to deal with the ever-mysterious 'spinning' and so on. It was rumoured that this pilot had frequently looped, and had even looped a B.E.2c.! We listened attentively, trying to pick up what crumbs we might from his learned conversation.

There had been talk of the test-pilot staying the night at Shoreham; he had landed because of the bad weather. But during the afternoon it cleared up considerably and the wind, although still strong, showed signs of abating. He decided to leave. We hurried down to the aerodrome to watch him go.

The beautiful machine was wheeled forward, her engine started, warmed up. The test-pilot and his civilian passenger donned much leather flying clothing, climbed into their seats. The engine having been run up and found satisfactory, the wooden chocks were removed, the machine turned and taxied out to the far side of the aerodrome. A short pause, and the pilot gave the engine full throttle, taking off obliquely towards the sheds.

Against the wind the machine rose at once and began to climb steeply. The pilot waved farewell as he passed us by, heading west into the sunlight. Against the bright sky the machine was silhouetted, hard to see beyond the end of the sheds. But, as we watched, shading our eyes, there came to us suddenly the spluttering of a starved engine. The steady roar of the exhaust died down, the nose of the machine dropped. And now this expert pilot made his great mistake.

In the course of the short flight, he had attained a height of about one hundred and fifty feet and had crossed the boundary of the aerodrome. A road, a line of telegraph wires were beneath him, ahead a series of small meadows intersected by ditches. Rough ground, but possible in an emergency, especially as the strong wind against him would make the run on landing exceptionally short. There was, strictly speaking, no alternative for a safe pilot. But this pilot was more than commonly skilful, and he wanted to save his new machine from damage. Not that it would have suffered anything worse than a broken undercarriage, possibly a smashed propeller, from the forced landing; he wished to avoid even that much. And so he tried something which, in this instance, he had not one chance in a thousand of bringing off. He turned back to the aerodrome.

In the very few seconds that followed I remember feeling, in spite of my ignorance of piloting, an intense admiration for the brilliant way in which he handled the machine. Without a moment's hesitation he turned down wind as quickly and as flatly as possible so as not to lose the little height he had, held a straight course for an instant, then over the sheds began another sharp turn that, when completed, would bring him into wind with a space of fifty or sixty yards of smooth ground on which to land. Actually it was just possible of achievement, although as I see it now he was taking a terrible risk; the whole performance was cut too fine.

As he came towards the sheds his speed down wind seemed terrific, yet in trying to maintain his height he had in fact lost the essential flying speed. He was stalling even as he banked over the sheds. The nose went down with a jerk in the first turn of a spin. He missed the roof by a miracle but within a second of the machine's disappearance behind the end shed we were horrified to hear an appalling crash.

Naturally we rushed forward in spite of the first-shouted order that all pupils should stand back—the sight of a probably fatal crash, it was rightly thought, might upset some of us—we *had* to see; we ran for it. Beyond the end shed the new aeroplane lay flat on the ground, a mass of wreckage. Both men sat in their smashed cockpits motionless. Unconscious or dead? We were not long in doubt for worse was to follow. As we came nearer the wreck about which mechanics were already trying to extricate the pilot and passenger, there was a flicker of fire from beneath the fuselage. And all at once the mechanics sprang back as with a roar a great flame shot up from the burst petrol tank. It swept back over the passenger; when it reached the pilot he moved uneasily, seemed to shake himself, fumbled with his safety-belt, then jumped out just in time, his clothing alight.

There were cries for extinguishers, for axes to hack through the broken wings, for help to pull away the wreckage, for the ambulance—for anything and everything to save the passenger. He was still in the machine and still alive. Mercifully he did not recover consciousness—afterwards it was found that his skull had been fractured in the crash—but he kept on moving. And we were powerless. The extinguishers had no effect upon thirty gallons of blazing petrol. The strong wind blew the flames into his face. Before our very eyes he was burnt to death, roasted. It took a long time; it was ghastly. . . .

The fire died down, smouldered awhile, went out. The wind dropped; the sun set and the sky glowed with rare beauty. But we pupils walked back to the mess in glum silence.

VI

Upon the following morning all attached officers were summoned to the Squadron Office. We expected the summons, although I don't quite know what we expected to hear. I suppose that, amongst other things, we thought to be given news of the pilot in hospital, possibly to be complimented upon the vain efforts we had made to penetrate the barrier of fire and upon the *sang-froid* we had shown afterwards. Perhaps more than anything we hoped to hear that the fire had not been so intense as our eyes had led us to believe, that the unfortunate passenger had in some way been protected— by his goggles, by his flying helmet or by his leather clothing —from the devouring fury of the flames, so that there might be a chance of his recovery. Or did we hope to be told that something very strange had gone wrong with this new aeroplane, something very startling and unusual which could not occur again, that flying was not like this, horrible, cruel?

The squadron-commander strode into the Office, flung his cap upon the table, drew a cane chair forward. Placing one foot upon the seat he rested an elbow on his knee.

'With regard to this unfortunate and unnecessary happening,' he began harshly, 'the first and only thing to do is to find out the causes of the accident, to see where the pilot was to blame so as to learn what lessons we may. Now in this particularly stupid case . . .'

I thought him terribly callous.

.   .   .   .   .

'A pilot must never turn down wind at a low altitude when faced with the possibility of a forced landing.

'A pilot in difficulties after leaving the ground must keep straight on and not attempt to turn back.

'A pilot must save himself and his passengers first, not the aeroplane. It is better to smash wheels and propeller than burn a man to death.

'A pilot must take particular care to maintain flying-speed after engine failure.'

Those were the lessons. If the manner of their teaching was hard, it was also effective.

VII

It was a long time between this accident and the start of my regular training in the air. After one preliminary flight many days passed before I was again taken up. Bad weather, too few machines and instructors, too many pupils, were the real causes of delay; but I began to fret and to wonder if discrimination rather than luck was not responsible for my name so seldom being called when the Longhorns stood in fantastic array upon the turf. I remembered the words heard on the evening of my arrival from the would-be adjutant; that little flying was done at Shoreham and that many pupils returned in disgust to their regiments. I had no intention of leaving the Flying Corps until I had had a fair chance of becoming a proficient pilot, but the slowness of the commencement was discouraging.

Nearly two weeks had gone by when one evening I was noticed as I stood disconsolate in front of the sheds. An instructor saw me and beckoned. We embarked in a Longhorn; I was given a flight lasting nearly half an hour. And after that things moved more quickly. Several days in succession were marked by flights either in the stillness of very early morning or in the calm of late afternoon. I began to know my way about a Longhorn. The forest of struts did not grow any thinner, but meaning and order came to it. It no longer took me minutes to thread an anxious path through the wires; I learnt to scramble quickly into my seat in the *nacelle* where the controls were at last becoming familiar. I was allowed to feel those controls while flying. After half a dozen flights I was even permitted to land and take off with only slight assistance from the instructor. In the air I could sense some connection, however vague, between the harmonium pedals working the rudder and the handlebars shaped like a pair of spectacles which gave lateral control. Presently I felt sure that I was making steady progress.

VIII

One cold grey morning a few of us were gathered upon the stretch of tarmac in front of the sheds expecting to enjoy that most exquisite of amusements, the sight of another's embarrassment, agony and discomfiture. One of our number, a man who had come to Shoreham before me and who had done considerably more flying, was to go for his first solo flight. He had been warned the night before, after half an hour in the air with the senior instructor.

'You'll go solo at dawn tomorrow,' he had been told briefly. And if for 'go solo' the words 'be shot' had been substituted he could not have been more upset.

Anxious though we were to be taken up for instruction, we hoped that first of all we should be permitted to witness the unfortunate man's departure. Secretly, I think we rather hoped that he would crash—not badly, we wished him no harm, but just enough to provide us with real entertainment.

Before one's own turn comes, one is apt to be merciless—
not only in aviation.

We were discussing the prospects of this little quiet fun
at another's expense, when the instructors came from the
office. One of them marched up to our group; as he passed
I caught his eye. He stopped. Ah-ha, I thought, this is
where I put in some more instructional flying. But the
Winged Hero was regarding me thoughtfully with something
in his eye that reminded me of a hungry tiger looking at
his meat.

'How much dual control have you done?' he asked.

'Three hours and twenty minutes,' I answered, hopeful
that so small an amount would induce him to give me
more at once.

'H'm . . .' he muttered, still looking at me fixedly. 'Do
you think you could go solo?'

The question staggered me. All my past lies flashed before me, whirled in my head and merged into one huge
thumping fib.

'Yes,' I answered, and at once regretted it.

'Very well then . . .' The instructor's voice was kind now,
like that of a surgeon about to announce the necessity for
a major operation. 'Very well, take up Longhorn Number
2965.'

Behind me there was titter of mirth, but it evoked no
response on my part. My hour had struck before I was pre-
pared. I knew nothing whatever about flying, and it was far
too early in the morning and it was cold and I hadn't had
breakfast. I was doomed and I knew it. I felt like asking for
a priest. . . . Walking blindly forward, I put on my flying cap.

Against the wings and struts of Longhorn Number 2965
mechanics were idly leaning. They made no move as I approached, gave me no more than a quick glance. They knew
well enough that I was a pupil, that unless I came to a
machine with an instructor there was nothing doing. But
when I began to clamber into the *nacelle* they stopped talking
and looked at one another uneasily.

'I am taking this machine up, Flight-Sergeant,' I announced
boldly.

There was a nasty sort of silence during which I felt
that behind my back signs were being made indicating

doubt of my sanity. At length I heard a subdued voice say, 'Very good, sir. Switch off?'

'Switch off,' I replied, nervously settling into the front seat of that *nacelle* which now seemed as lonely as an autocrat's throne. At my back whispering mechanics turned the propeller. 'Contact?' came a voice like that of an undertaker.

For a moment I gave myself up to the wild and wonderful hope that the engine was not going to start. They had to pull it round twice. And then it clitter-clattered into life and I knew that I was 'for it'. Adjusting the throttle to slowest running, I stared round fearfully at the collection of struts, tail-booms and spars that had once again resolved itself into a dense forest in which I would presently be as lost as any Babe in the Wood. Through wire entanglements I caught sight of two mechanics grinning at me. Horrible ghouls, gloating over my forthcoming demise! Was there no way out? I turned my face to the morning sky where the light was still growing. Like the tenor in *Tosca* I had never loved life so much. Not a breath of wind anywhere, save the slight draught of the slowly revolving propeller. I sniffed the air, and inspiration came to me. Perhaps if I got out of the *nacelle* and strolled nonchalantly over to the sheds murmuring, 'No lift in the air,' I should be granted a reprieve. I looked hopefully over the side. Below stood the instructor.

'Get well out across the aerodrome before you take off,' he said. 'And don't taxi too fast.'

I nodded, speechless, and buckled up the safety-belt.

IX

In those days the newspapers still occasionally referred to an aeroplane pilot as 'the intrepid rider', and upon the instant when Longhorn and I rose gently into the air I came to know that the expression referred to me. I was intrepid whether I liked it or not. And I was certainly a rider. I squatted rigidly upright upon the edge of my elevated seat, holding the handlebars delicately between forefinger and thumb, treading the rudder pedals as though I were walking upon unbroken eggs. Behind me the alarm-clocks ticked relentlessly; ahead that tea-tray of an elevator held not only my gaze but all my hopes of surviving the adventure.

Ah, that forward elevator, what a blessing it was! It gave one something to look at, something to guide one in keeping the nose of the machine at the right level. If you kept it on or just below the horizon you were safe—until the time came to make a turn. Then you put the nose down lower still. Never make a level turn, still less a climbing one—that was bound to be fatal. Before putting on any bank push the stick forward a little to increase the speed. . . . I was remembering my lessons, anxiety was diminishing. I looked quickly about me. Everything seemed to be all right. But it would not last unless I continued to be very, very careful. I glued my eyes to the front elevator.

Presently, without daring to move my head, I rolled my eyes towards the instruments. The altimeter was recording something. I was indeed off the ground: nearly four hundred feet! It was exhilarating at this altitude. But only momentarily so; I had to get back. My wrist-watch showed that I had been in the air for no less than three minutes. Underneath the elevator, Worthing pier was beginning to come close. Yes, I had to get back! Without great skill this first turn would be my last. . . .

Nose down; a slight movement of the handlebars; the machine banked slowly. Softest pressure of the foot; she began to turn. I repeated my lessons over the sea. 'Beware of stalling. Beware of spinning. Don't push the nose down too far, or you'll strain the engine or pull the wings off or something. Gently does it!' The bungalows of Shoreham came in sight. 'Now—off rudder, off bank—steady! Level up, watching the elevator. And watch the speed-gauge too. Fifty-three miles an hour? Oh, that's far too much! Up with the nose—gently—just a ve-ry lee-tle. There!' I had completed my first turn.

The aerodrome came towards me again, passed by directly underneath. I risked a glance over the side. There was quite a crowd of pupils on the tarmac. They were staring up, watching me; I was on my first solo and it was proving to be successful! But I was not home yet and pride comes before a fall. . . . The speed indicator showed thirty-eight. Too slow! Down with the nose—but *gently*. Unless I was gentle as a nursing mother something dreadful would happen. I would spin into the ground and wake up to find, at the best, wings very different from those I coveted sprouting from between my shoulder-blades.

Not far from Brighton I made my second turn and headed back into wind. Then over Shoreham town I pushed the nose firmly down and pulled back the throttle. Longhorn commenced to glide towards the aerodrome. The air-speed settled down to a steady forty-two. I had entered the last phase.

In the very early days machines used to be flown down with the engine almost full out, a procedure considered necessary to maintain flying-speed. Of course the majority of the early aviators never had to come down from any very great height or they would have found it a tiresome business, but the first time that a pilot (whose engine, it so happened, had failed at a considerable altitude) *glided* down to his landing something new and wonderful was discovered. The French called it a *vol plané*, the British Press a 'Death Dive'. It was that morbid expression which I remembered as the Longhorn bore me earthwards.

Not that I found gliding unpleasant, far from it. It was the prospect of landing that I dreaded. All had gone well so far. Longhorn was still intact, making a happy rustling sound as she sailed slowly through the calm air. On the green surface of the aerodrome the sun shone, the wind rippled the long grass. But what was going to happen when these two met, the aeroplane and the aerodrome? I was sure I could never bring myself—alone, unaided—to 'flatten out' at just the right moment. There would not be much noise, I thought; a heavy crunch and then struts, spars, wires, white fabric would all collapse and fold themselves about me. I would remain sitting in the crushed *nacelle* until they sent a party from the sheds to liberate me; and their laughter would be restrained only if I were seriously hurt.

Meanwhile the ground seemed to be coming up in normal fashion. The broad river curving towards the sea glinted darkly, momentous as the Rubicon. But Longhorn did not falter; she crossed it, and was at just the right height on passing the tall bank at the eastern side of the aerodrome. The sun still shone. I could see the daisies in the grass beneath me. Time to flatten out. With the utmost gentleness I pulled

back the handlebars, treading nervously on the harmonium
pedals to bring the nose dead into wind. The front elevator
rose, the noise of the wind in the wires died away. I stared
ahead like a hypnotised rabbit. From directly underneath
there came a hollow rumble, from further astern a scraping
sound; the machine shook, gave a gentle lurch. My heart
rose to my throat with alarm. What was happening? Still
keeping my head rigidly to the front I squinted down at
the speed indicator. Nothing! At the altimeter—Zero. . . . I
looked boldly over the side. The grass was very near, almost
motionless. I could see each blade. Fuzz from a dandelion
blew slowly past the lower plane. I had landed.

As I taxied back to the sheds two mechanics came out to
guide the machine in. They were still grinning. Never have
I seen smiles of such seraphic beauty.

'How did you get on?' a fellow pupil asked.

'Oh, all right,' I answered carelessly. 'But—not much lift
in the air.'

X

Not many days later a number of us were transferred at
short notice to Gosport, to complete our training and to be
attached to a new squadron then being formed. The transfer
was something of a move up, but to me it was also very
alarming. I had got the hang of things at Shoreham; I had
done some half a dozen solo flights, I knew the instructors
and their ways, I was at home in two different Longhorns,
and I had learnt to find my way about the country within
a radius of as much as three miles in the air. What was going
to happen at Gosport? Would the new instructors understand me or I them? Would they fly in the same manner?
Would their machines be the same? There were many different types at Gosport; would I be expected to fly them all?
If I were not taken up again soon I might forget the little
I had learnt. The very air might be different; it might not
have as much lift as at Shoreham. It was all very disquieting.

And indeed for the first few days at the new station I was
not altogether happy. The quarters were uncomfortable, my
kit had not arrived, the place was overcrowded, and over-

Maurice Farman Longhorn—the type of aircraft on which the author learnt to fly in 1915.

B.E.2c, the RFC's all-purpose aircraft of 1915

Shorthorn assaulting a German balloon, October 1915. *Painting by James Leech*

crowded not only with pupils but with a lot of people who already had their 'Wings' and would scarcely speak to the novices. Worst of all when I arrived there was only one Longhorn available for training; a queue waited to fly her.

There were also, it is true, a couple of Shorthorns, but my log-book showed that I had not yet been up in one and the shortage of instructors prevented my being given the necessary dual-control flights. The trouble with a Shorthorn was that it had no nice tea-tray elevator in front with which to judge the correct flying angle, and thus the first impression to a Longhorn pilot was quite frightening, as if he were hanging out recklessly over a balcony. I stationed myself close to the only Longhorn and pestered everyone who came by to let me take her up.

In this way I managed to get in an occasional flight, accomplished safe landings, broke nothing. But progress was distressingly slow. I began to think that perhaps I was fated to remain a Longhorn pilot all my days; at times I even hoped so, for some of the other machines at Gosport were rather terrifying. There were B.E.s of various categories—and the last B.E. I had seen had been the burning wreck at Shoreham—there were Caudrons with powerful 80 horsepower 'Gnome' engines, Blériot monoplanes, Martinsyde scouts and many others. All seemed wonderfully fast, modern, powerful, and all a trifle dangerous to the eye of a novice.

One fine evening after I had completed a practice flight in the Longhorn, a friendly young instructor took me over to look at a Caudron from close quarters. She was a nice little machine with engine and propeller in front, a small boat-shaped body for two people, and wooden tail-booms running back to the elevator and rudders. She could do about sixty miles an hour when hard pressed.

The instructor climbed up, inviting me into the passenger seat in front of him. It was a bit cramped and I did not at all like the way a piece of cowling, removed to let me enter, was bolted down behind me to prevent my falling out. I was afraid that if the machine crashed that front seat would become a death trap. But I said nothing and a moment later the engine was started.

B

I held my breath as we took off, but except for the engine smelling abominably and making a great deal of noise (it was the first time I had flown behind a rotary engine) I enjoyed the flight thoroughly. I was with an excellent pilot and I felt quite safe after all in the front seat. This was, for me, a new type of aeroplane, a new experience about which I would be able to talk in the mess. All too soon it was over. I was rather surprised when we landed in the middle of the aerodrome and when, turning round, I saw the pilot getting out of his seat although the engine was still running. I unbolted the cowling at my back and started to get out too, thinking that perhaps something had gone wrong and that I could help. But by now the pilot was standing on the grass, buzzing the engine on and off by means of a switch at the side of the body. He signed to me not to get down but to climb into the pilot's seat.

'Try the controls,' he said between buzzes.

I tried them. They seemed all right. Lateral control was by 'warping' the wing instead of by aileron; it seemed rather stiff, but I supposed that very little would be necessary for normal bank. The rudder control was much lighter.

'She needs a bit of left rudder in the air,' the pilot remarked. 'And you can leave the throttle control there'—he indicated the position—'all the time you're flying, but hold on to it. Cut it down a little when you want to glide, and use your thumb-switch. Understand?'

I nodded intelligently, thinking it all over and trying to remember some of it for future reference.

'All right,' he went on, 'don't stay up for more than twenty minutes. Off you go!'

'Off I go?' I repeated, unable to believe my ears.

He wagged his head cheerfully and let go of the switch. The machine began to move forward.

I cried out anxiously.

'But—I say . . .' The engine was making a horrible noise and I had forgotten where the switch was. The pilot did not hear me.

'Don't forget,' he shouted as he skipped out of the way of the tail-booms, 'don't forget that she stalls at forty-two!'

I stared forward helplessly, hopelessly. The machine was bumping about over a stretch of uneven ground, swinging

wildly from side to side. Which rudder had he told me to use?
Left or right? I tried each in turn, gradually discovering
how to keep the nose straight while fumbling around with
my left hand to find the switch. My fingers encountered
the throttle lever; more by less or chance I pushed it forward
to the very position the instructor had indicated. The engine
roared with satisfaction. The tail came off the ground, I felt
myself being lifted in my seat. Instinctively—already it was
becoming an instinct!—I eased back the control stick to
prevent the machine from falling on her nose. The bumping
and bounding suddenly ceased—merciful heavens, I was
off the ground!

My immediate reaction was one of far greater apprehen-
sion than I had experienced upon my first solo. Then, for all
my ignorance, I had really been quite comfortable in a Longhorn seat. Now everything was unfamiliar. I could not
see ahead; there was a flame-spitting, whirling mass of
cylinders and propeller in front of the frail boat in which I
squirmed. And wherever I looked there seemed to be struts
or wings to obscure the view—except of the departing
earth. I held the stick firmly in what I judged to be a neutral
position and watched the speed gauge.

I found the switch at last, but now I deemed it wiser to
go on. I had very little spare flying-speed. If I tried to land
I should come down like a cast-iron pancake, smashing the
machine to match-wood. Besides, there was a line of trees
ahead—about the only thing I *could* see—somehow I would
have to get over them before finding safety. No use getting
upset, I had to make a circuit of the aerodrome if I wanted
to live to tell that young instructor what I thought of him.
Clutching desperately at the throttle and stick I was borne
aloft, thinking upon Elijah.

Compared to a Longhorn this Caudron was speedy and
climbed remarkably fast. In no more than ten minutes I
had reached a height of one thousand feet. She seemed to
be climbing too fast. I peered hastily at the speed gauge.
It was very hard to see, for the cockpit was dark and my
eyes were half blinded by the sunset (probably my last)
over the Solent towards which I was being unwillingly
carried. At what speed, I wondered, had that man told me
she would stall? Was it forty-two? Anyway, I was taking

no risks. Well above forty-five for me. I pushed the stick farther forward—*Trial by Jury* was then playing in Portsmouth, a line slightly parodied came into my head in tune with the engine's beat:

> 'She might very well stall at forty-five,
> In the dusk with the light behind her.'

The light was certainly behind the instruments; I had to guess my speed by the feel of the machine, a lesson it was just as well I should learn then and there. Dusk? Yes, that was coming; unless I hurried the light would be bad for landing. I should bounce like a tennis ball. I tried a turn. It succeeded better than I had hoped. And of a sudden I felt a new confidence coming to me. This was fine, this was real flying, better than a Longhorn. I made another turn. The light was on the instruments now, I felt much happier. Height two thousand feet, speed fifty-one, revolutions per minute, one thousand and fifty; everything smooth and comfortable. I looked out of the boat and down.

Fort Grange was directly underneath; the aerodrome a little to my left. Ahead the houses of Gosport; in the distant Portsmouth lights were already beginning to twinkle in the streets. I throttled down, buzzing the engine to keep the propeller turning. The machine glided slowly but extraordinarily steeply, I found; it was so nearly a dive that I watched the ground over the top plane. The summer air grew pleasantly warmer as I came lower, and greatly daring I essayed a turn on the glide. It was easier than I had thought, for there was not a bump or a pocket in the air on this quiet August evening.

Above the sheds, still a good fifty feet up, I straightened out, began calculating my landing point. A sidelong glance at the tarmac showed me the young instructor looking up from among a group of other pilots. He was very tall and therefore known as 'Tiny'. I hoped that he was proud of his pupil. I felt angry no more. Rather I wanted to laugh and shake him by the hand. I was glad that he had had confidence enough in my abilities to send me off upon this delightful machine....

The landing held all my thoughts. Shakily I buzzed the

engine as though sending out an S O S, drew the stick back gently, gradually, guessing the distance to the ground. The rush of wind died away; the nose came up steadily; the tail sank. I looked at the air-speed: dangerously near to the fatal forty-two mark, then just under. The machine sank a little, slowing down. And but for the rumbling of the wheels and the scratch of the tail-booms over stones beneath the grass, I should not have known that I had landed.

XI

There followed a spell of exceptionally fine weather, during which I was sent up two or three times every day for short flights on the Caudron, the Longhorn, or occasionally on one of the Shorthorns. But in spite of my new confidence I was still very cautious in the air, and on the ground I found myself always listening for useful hints that might be dropped by those Winged Heroes, the fully-fledged pilots. There were plenty of minor crashes, but none so ghastly or so close to me as that first one at Shoreham, and I fancy that those of us who had survived the moral effect of that disaster were no longer much disturbed by other people's misfortunes. And yet some of the mysterious happenings to experienced aviators filled me every now and then with anxiety for the future. There was a limit it seemed to the wisdom of even the best pilots; what on earth—or in the air—could I be expected to do in circumstances with which they themselves did not know how to deal?

The newly forming squadron at Gosport was to be equipped with B.E.2c aeroplanes. A pilot whom I knew and liked was sent to bring one from a depot near London. When he landed he became at once the centre of an admiring crowd, for the B.E. with its latest improvements and its 90 horse-power engine was a novelty and highly thought of. The pilot gave a half-humorous account of his flight.

'It was very bumpy over Winchester,' he announced, 'and the dirty beast tried to spin on me!'

Exclamations of interest were followed by many questions. How had it started? What was it like, how serious had it been, what had he done to correct it? His answers were calmly given, but they were not very clear. I at least could gather nothing from them; a spin remained something mysterious and deadly, a danger from which there was no salvation, which attacked one suddenly and for no reason in mid-air. I must watch for signs of that spin as a traveller through unexplored country might watch for a savage ambush.

The little Caudron, however, was perfectly safe; she had never been known to spin. Providing one did not stall her, she would give no trouble. She was strong, had a low landing-speed, required a comparatively short run for taking off and was more or less fool-proof in the air. Her one weakness was that whirling incinerator of an engine. But in spite of occasional trouble, I developed a great affection for the little machine. In her I made my first long cross-country flights and enjoyed my first two forced landings. I say 'enjoyed' retrospectively, because I managed to bring them both off successfully, not because I was at all happy at the time they occurred.

XII

It happened one day that, when I was about to leave on a cross-country flight in the Caudron, a letter had to be delivered urgently to a senior officer at that moment inspecting the reserve squadron at Shoreham. With some formality and many cautions not to tarry on the way, I was entrusted with the despatch.

To say that I was pleased to revisit in so smart a machine the scene of my first trembling solo would be far short of the truth. It mattered not to me that the despatch was of no real importance and that a copy was being sent by post; at being selected to perform this mission I was elated as if I had been promoted two steps in rank. It was a glorious morning, the engine sang a crackling paean of triumph; I flew via Fareham, Chichester, Arundel and Lancing. After much climbing, the Caudron reached a height of four thousand feet; below me small puffs of cloud drifted slowly astern. I felt rather reckless in thus flying above them, they gave such an impression of altitude; but I was beginning to know the look of the country from the air. I could distinguish between a railway and a river, between forests and factory chimneys.

Everything went well on the way out and I reached Shoreham in good time, looking down proudly before commencing the glide. Some of the less fortunate pupils of my day were still being taught here. I fancied I could discern one or two of them in the drooping Longhorns slowly circling the aerodrome. I switched off and dived earthwards —dived, because gliding in a Caudron, except that it was delightfully slow, resembled in angle of descent the 'Death Dive' of the newspapers. Over the sheds I buzzed the engine a good deal and did one gentle turn of a spiral so as to make sure of having an audience, then straightening out, came lower and—glory be!—made a very decent landing.

To complete the impression of efficiency I taxied in very fast, and in a Caudron that meant with the tail off the ground to avoid the braking effect of the tail-booms in the grass. More by luck than by good judgment, I switched off in the nick of time, fetching up on the edge of the tarmac, my propeller almost touching a Longhorn's rudder. A few yards away a group of officers stood watching; I spied my senior officer amongst them. Wishing to complete my performance as smartly as possible, I sprang lightly from the pilot's seat, forgot the control wires which ran aft to the tail, and tripping over a cable fell flat on my face. I began to regret that all the pupils were now assembled in front of the sheds; I could see wide grins on several familiar faces. However, picking myself up I limped clear of the Caudron with a barked shin, and hastened to deliver my despatch to the senior officer. He smiled, thanked me warmly; and when he added that I had made a very nice landing and that he hoped I had not hurt myself, I felt as proud as though I were the dying patriot reporting to the Emperor at Ratisbon.

In the mess they treated me as if I already had my Wings. Even the No-lift-in-the-air motor salesman (*still* there) deigned talk with me. I told him the Caudron was very apt to spin.

XIII

But upon the return journey I paid for the pride and joy of the morning. I had had a swim and an excellent lunch; had I been my own master I should also have had a short *siesta*. When at length I soared into the air, watched by a crowd of envious pupils, and set course for Gosport I felt —for the first time in my life in an aeroplane—really happy, almost drowsy. The engine no longer seemed to emit a menacing roar, but rather to hum a regular, slightly monotonous lullaby. The air had all the requisite 'lift' in it, there were no bumps, it was warm even at two thousand five hundred feet and the sky was cloudless all the way to Gosport. I leaned back, very nearly at my ease.

On the way home I followed the seashore to see from the air a coast I had long known on the ground. Ahead, Hayling Island came gradually into my ken. I had done a course in machine-gunnery there before joining the Flying Corps and I thought that I would like to look more closely at so familiar a locality. After passing over it I should, of course, have to turn inland to avoid the prohibited area of Portsmouth; that would involve quite a long detour by Fareham. But there was plenty of time before sunset; the evening was calm, clear, and of such beauty as to make the temptation to stay up a little longer irresistible to a young airman.

Presently I was above marshes and mudflats and the arms of the quiet sea encircling the island. I began to recognise roads, lanes, cottages, clumps of trees, to see paths down which I had so often marched, open stretches across which I had rushed perspiring with weighty pieces of Vickers or Lewis guns. I smiled contentedly from the superior position to which I had advanced. . . . Perhaps it was overconfidence that did it. I don't know. At all events there was a sudden change of note in the engine's steady music, then a slowing down and much vibration. From rhythmical roaring the explosions dwindled until they were like nothing more than a faint crackling of ice in a cocktail-shaker. Then they ceased altogether. The silence seemed immense. And with it came a nasty pain in the pit of my stomach: alone, two thousand feet up, an amateur pilot, and no engine! This must be the end. I fumbled around desperately;

wiggled the throttle lever, tried the switch, buried my head
in the cockpit to see if the petrol was properly turned on,
fumbled some more.

When I took my head out of the cockpit I found that the
noise of wind in the wings and wires had unaccountably
died away. The rudder bar and control stick seemed strangely
easy to move. And the nose of the machine was dropping
heavily, uncontrollably. . . . Heavens, I had lost flying-speed!
I was stalling—about to spin? Without thinking I pushed
the stick hard forward. The Caudron gathered speed; and
within two seconds I was sighing my relief, wind had come
back to the wires, feeling to the controls. I flattened to a
more normal glide and began to do some quick thinking.

What were my lessons? 'Keep straight on, don't lose
flying-speed.' Well, after a moment's panic I was doing
that all right. The next step? 'Make sure of the direction
of the wind.' At Shoreham I had been heading directly into
it, how was it here? I gazed earthwards. There was a ripple
of air over the cornfields, too erratic to be a sure guide.
A herd of cows was obstinately refusing to obey the laws
of bovine nature, for not two faced the same way. No sailing
craft at sea, no flags on the houses. Ah, smoke from a
cottage chimney! I had never seen household smoke as
friendly. Country people should always let their chimneys
smoke to help poor airmen in distress. I took the wind's
bearing with precision, turned into it at once. Now? 'Choose
the field in which you intend to land, and choose it as early
as you can.' A glance at the altimeter—less than fifteen hundred feet—in alarm I hung over the side, goggling at the
earth. Choose? Not so easy. There were innumerable fields,
but only a few large enough. I examined those few attentively.
Marshes! Or else green mud from which the tide had receded.
. . . Under a thousand feet now. No time to lose.

At last, just in time, I found it. The only smooth bit of
pasture, it seemed, for miles, but not so very smooth at
that. A sort of paddock, small, enclosed on three sides by
trees, with a tall hedge upon my side. 'Aim at the hedge
on the near side,' I had been taught. I did so and found
that I was too high. Another lesson came back to me: 'If
you think you are going to overshoot make "S"-turns so as to
lose height.' I did so. In the middle of the second turn the

engine all at once started again. If it had happened any higher up I might have tried to continue the flight, with unfortunate results for a second later it stopped for good. However, low down it only served to remind me of one more lesson: 'Always switch off before a forced landing, to minimise the risk of fire.' I knocked up the switch immediately. Fire? The field was small and the trees very close; I might crash and crash badly, but I refused to burn. I could remember no more lessons, there was no time to think of anything else. The machine hopped over the hedge; I commenced shakily to flatten out.

The landing was not too bad, although rather fast—a better fault than stalling!—and all would have been well but for a partly filled in drainage ditch concealed by the grass. I was staring ahead, wondering whether I should be able to stop before hitting the trees on the far side of the field, when there came a heavy bump beneath the wheels. The machine swerved, listed to port, and came to a sudden stop.

It took me a few moments to recover my wits in the surprising stillness of the summer's evening here on the ground. It seemed very wrong of me to have thus brusquely disturbed the dignified quiet of this sweet-smelling field. Then I scrambled out to inspect the damage. It was nothing much. A wheel had been broken in the ditch, a steel undercarriage strut twisted. It could all easily be repaired on the spot. . . .

Solicitous inhabitants crowded round, offering help, advice, congratulations, food and drink, shelter for the night, a guard for the machine. I asked for a telephone. This was the first time I had broken anything since starting to fly, and now that the anguish of the descent was past I wondered ruefully whether the breaking of a wheel would not put a black mark against my name. From the nearest house I 'phoned through to Gosport.

The orderly-officer to whom I spoke was non-committal, he told me to stay where I was and that perhaps help would be forthcoming on the morrow. Then he rang off. I passed an uneasy night despite hospitable surroundings. . . .

But upon the next day, back at Gosport with the repaired Caudron, they said I had not managed so badly for a beginner—although they refused to believe that I had not got a girl hidden away on Hayling Island. No one, they said, would land there for less than that.

XIV

These ugly rumours were soon dispelled. Another and much longer cross-country flight in the same Caudron resulted in a second forced landing, this time near Winchester. And not only was it generally agreed by the pilots of Gosport that, with Portsmouth so close, it would be silly to have a girl in Winchester, but the condition of the 'Gnome' engine revealed on examination that I could not have flown another yard in any direction.

I had broken nothing on this landing and I was now considered advanced enough to pilot the famous B.E.2c. As a matter of fact I am not quite sure whether the machine I flew at Gosport was a '2c' or some other earlier category. It had a less powerful engine—an 80 horse-power Renault —cables instead of streamline wires, and wooden skids on the undercarriage. Altogether a less modern craft than the ill-fated machine I had seen burned at Shoreham, which had been of the type just coming into fashion.

But despite some preliminary nervousness due to the rumours of spinning, I soon began to like the B.E. as much and more than the other types I had flown. She was stable, easily manageable if a bit heavy on the controls, strongly built. One of the more experienced of the Gosport pilots had been known to loop his B.E. several times and no harm done, although he had not been allowed to repeat the performance in front of the novices lest we should be tempted to emulate him, which, frankly, was not very likely. After a few practice flights in this type of machine I was allowed to take up my first passengers, luckless young men who little knew into what trembling hands they had trusted their lives. Also I was allowed to fly in windy, bumpy weather that hitherto had been the signal for machines to be securely locked in their sheds for the day. . . . I flew over the New Forest, circling above lonely heaths and dark glades and gypsy encampments, retracing a hundred boyhood rides. I flew over the Solent and peered into the secret places

of that shallow sea whose waters roll over my early dreams.
I learned to fly a straight course by compass and to make
allowances for the wind; I learned how to bank at 45 degrees,
and how to do a spiral glide from a height of several thousand
feet. The war? It seemed far away, but I would be in it soon
enough.

XV

On the ground, during all this time, instruction in rigging
and engine fitting went steadily on; occasionally we were given
vaguely scientific lectures upon aerodynamics. And at length
the great day arrived. A few of us who were deemed worthy
were driven off in a Crossley tender to the Central Flying
School at Upavon to be examined in our knowledge of aeronautics.

That the tests were not entirely easy was a matter of
common knowledge. If we passed we would be qualified
pilots, if we failed we would be set back many weeks, perhaps months. Failure was by no means unknown. In my own
case it happened that I was a little ahead of the customary
time, but there were only two things I had cause to dread:
that I might not yet have enough flying hours to my credit
or—much worse—that I should not have sufficiently mastered the Morse code, a thing which for years had tried my
patience. We were required to read messages at a fair speed,
so many words a minute. My average rate was so many
minutes per word. All the way to Upavon I practised with
a portable buzzer.

The examination started as soon as we had disembarked,
and I quickly found that it was less terrifying than I had
been led to expect. I was conducted round the sheds by a
venerable naval airman—anything over thirty with pre-war
flying experience was considered venerable—who asked all
the hard questions of which I had had warning and who
seemed surprised that I could also answer the easy ones.
Another old gentleman—his hair was grey at the temples—
took me to the repair shops and asked me what most generally went wrong with 'Gnome' engines. From personal
experience with the Caudron I was able to tell him quite a

lot of things in the manner of an expert, and I gathered from his friendly smile that I had scored a good mark. Then came the Morse. In a darkened shed a nasty little lamp flashed irritatingly before my dazed eyes. Pencil and paper were handed to me; I made a pretence of scrawling. And to my amazement the dots and dashes assembled themselves in the correct order. The letters, even the words came out right. But I must have been helped by some guardian angel, for never again was I able to repeat the performance.

The dreaded business was over. In the cool of the evening we motored home, singing and occasionally stopping at a wayside pub to drink to our own success.

XVI

Before leaving Upavon I had made fairly sure that I had qualified, but the official result was not announced at Gosport until a day or two later. At length the news came through. I was summoned to the squadron office to hear it. The squadron-commander beamed, offered congratulations. I was no more a fledgeling, he said, I was a pilot, a member of the Corps, entitled to wear the badge and uniform, *sic itur ad astra* and so on. But to me it meant even more than that. I felt that I was no longer temporarily 'attached' to the Flying Corps; I was permanently devoted.

In a momentarily serious frame of mind I hurried from the office and across the sunlit barrack square of Fort Grange. Barely six weeks previously, at Shoreham, I had seen a man burnt to death because of a pilot's error. Since then I had learned to fly. I had made no fatal errors so far, I must see to it that I made none in the future. I had been taught all the essential lessons. Now to apply them.

In the tailor's shop I watched a man sew the Wings to my tunic. When it was done I went to the sheds and had the old training machine brought out. By my orders and upon my responsibility she was started up. As soon as she was ready I took her into the air. For half an hour I flew steadily and, in a Longhorn, for the last time.

2

The Wings Are Spread

I

I had hoped to fly out to France as a member of one of the new squadrons, but it was not to be. At short notice a number of us were ordered overseas by boat and train. In the dawn of a September morning we came to St Omer.

At the railway station no one knew anything; elsewhere in the town men slept. There were five of us in the party, all pilots; we routed round the nearby offices together. From a sleepy N.C.O. we gathered the information that there was nothing doing until after nine o'clock, but he told us of a café that would be open, to which we repaired and ate omelettes uneasily, disturbed by a distant rumbling of guns that seemed to be calling us forward away from this strange inactivity.

St Omer was headquarters of the Flying Corps as well of the army in France. The fact was known to the world, yet in the town itself the secret was closely guarded and we could find no one to guide us. At length we tried the telephone; to good purpose, but it was nearly ten o'clock before we reported to the Flying Corps' château. Then things went a little more rapidly. Too many pilots had collected during the past few days, there was no room in the château, no room at the aerodrome or anywhere else in the vicinity. Rather regretfully we were informed that we should have to be sent on at once to squadrons at the front. We sighed our polite relief and bundled into the inevitable Crossley.

A couple of hours later we were in the town of Aire, reporting to wing headquarters. More delay. The wing château was a place of dingy refinement. We were shown into a little *salon* that had all the feel of a dentist's waiting-room, including the month-old papers. The doors were firmly closed behind us—I was afraid that they were locked until I tried them—and for a while there was silence, save for that mutter of gunfire grown closer. Unconsciously we talked in whispers, starting guiltily whenever some stern-visaged staff officer peeped in to glance at us as though we were exhibits in a morgue. There were a few books apart from the papers; I dipped into a life of Wellington (left about for the guidance of young officers?), wondering what he would have done or said. Here, nobody seemed to want any of us.

We lunched in the same *salon*, the wing transport-officer honouring us with his presence. Of the wing-commander we saw nothing. There were Indian troops in the neighbour-hood, perhaps he had adopted their caste system. Towards four o'clock however there was a slight stir in an adjoining office; we were summoned forth and released from the sunbaked stuffiness of the house. In silence we re-embarked in the Crossley. The transport-officer, smiling mysteriously, saw us off. The driver alone seemed to know of our desti-nation.

It was hot, motoring. The dusty roads slipped by beneath shady avenues or between the gently undulating fields of northern France. Two pilots were dropped off at a drowsy village near which was said to be an aerodrome. We could see no signs of it and they set out to find it for themselves. A little further on two more pilots departed; I was left alone on the front seat with the taciturn driver.

Heading north-east, we passed through Merville, alive as on a peace-time market day. The voice of the guns was like thunder now, but the countryside was heavy with peace. Hindus bathed and washed in a stream by the roadside. A great wagon laden with forage came towards us and, although the men beside it wore khaki, the stout hairy-heeled draught-horses might have been cut from a print after Morland, and the sweet scent of hay lingered long after our passage. I grew sleepy from the quiet drive; my head was nodding when we turned from the main road to bump over a deeply rutted track.

I rubbed my eyes and sat up straight. By the side of
a russet farmhouse a line of motor lorries was drawn up.
Beyond canvas tents, poplars cast long shadows across a
reed-grown canal. The Crossley came to a stop. In the farmhouse I found the offices of my new squadron.

II

The Flying Corps seemed to have a knack of finding
varied, even picturesque, quarters. At Shoreham we had
lived in railway carriages more or less artistically converted
into bungalows; at Gosport I had occupied a dugout in a
dismantled fort; here the mess and accommodation for
more than half the squadron was in a barge floating upon
the canalised River Lys.

From the farmhouse I found my own way to the barge
past workshop lorries, stores tents, transport lines. There
were very few officers about and the one or two I met were
strangely distant, offhand, unwilling or unable to speak.
Near the river I met one who so far broke the ice as to ask
me to which Flight I had been posted. I told him, and in
reply he nodded down the river-bank to a line of canvas
hangars. 'There's your flight-commander,' he said.

Glad to know of someone to whom I had a legitimate
right to speak, I hurried off.

'Come from Gosport have you?' he remarked when I
had explained my presence. 'H'm—how much flying have you
done?'

'Thirty-three and a half hours.'

'How much?' he exclaimed, but he meant 'how little'.
And he went on to declare violently that it was a disgrace
to send pilots to a squadron on active service who did not
have fifty, no, a hundred hours to their credit. What types
had I flown? Longhorn? Of course, but that was no damn'
use! Caudron? Good Lord—that was worse than nothing!
Ah, so I had flown a B.E., had I? What sort of a B.E.?
Not the latest type, with the new undercarriage and the
90 horse-power 'R.A.F.' engine? No? Well then—no good.
A Shorthorn? So I had actually had the goodness to fly a
Shorthorn. Well, I should fly more of them here. 'And stand

to attention when I'm speaking to you,' he concluded sharply. 'And salute when you wish to address me and call me "sir", and put your cap on straight!'—or words very much to that effect.

I slunk wretchedly away, wishing myself dead and decently buried. No wonder people spoke of the horrors of war, this flight-commander must be one of them. Later on I discovered that he was not such a bad fellow as he made himself out to be, although addicted to the three 'R's'—Raving, Ranting and Remorse. But at the time I was thoroughly crestfallen; joining this squadron was worse than being a new boy at school. Boarding the barge, I went to hide my shame in the little cabin which had been allotted to me.

After seeing to the disposal of my kit I sallied forth boldly to look at the sheds and aerodrome, or rather to look *for* the aerodrome; I had seen nothing so far that could be given so large a name. Walking along the river-bank I encountered near the canvas sheds a pilot and an observer. They stared at me and passed on without a word. I looked into one of the sheds. It contained a Shorthorn, a rather tired-looking machine with the extensions of the upper plane folded downwards for want of space. Some mechanics were working on her, in silence. I went on to the next shed; another Shorthorn and my flight-commander were in it alone. I backed out hurriedly, saluting. The flight-commander gazed at me thoughtfully, chewing a piece of straw, but he said nothing. People in England did not know all the truth; the navy was not the only Silent Service. I began to wonder whether I had not by some chance strayed into a colony of Trappists.

But whereas until then I had been willing to talk to anyone about anything, the aerodrome—so called—left me speechless. Roughly it was shaped like the letter L, but the upright stroke was barely one hundred yards long by twenty wide, while the horizontal stroke following the curve of the Lys was perhaps two hundred and fifty yards in length and varied in width from about a hundred feet at the far end to no more than forty in front of the sheds. The angle where the two strokes met was rough ground sloping down to the riverside at the barge's mooring-place. On the far side of the river stood a line of tall poplars, elsewhere there were hedges, ditches, farm buildings and aeroplane hangars. The short stroke of the L could plainly not be used unless there happened to be a strong and favourable wind; the main stretch seemed scarcely better. As a temporary and concealed landing-ground the place had little enough in its favour, but as the permanent base of a busy squadron I have still not the slightest doubt that it was one of the least suitable spots for an aerodrome in all the flat country of north-eastern France.

On the other hand, there was no denying that from the officers' latrines, which I next visited, the view of plough-land, lush grass meadows, reeds bending over still water, slender poplars, high red-tiled farm gables, the whole scene backed by a wooden horizon and cloud-flecked sky, was perfect in the best manner of the old Dutch masters. Whoever selected that aerodrome may very well have been an artist, he was certainly not a pilot.

On my way back to the barge I fell in with the flight-commander. He had an unpleasant way of materialising like some grotesque character from *Alice*. I was not quite sure which one, but it was not the Cheshire Cat for I missed the reassuring grin. 'Growl,' I thought, would be an appropriate name for him.

'Did you say that you *had* flown Shorthorns?' he asked in a more kindly tone than he had previously used. I told him respectfully that I had indeed had that pleasure.

'Lucky for you,' he answered gloomily, 'that's all I've got in my Flight at present. You'll have to hang around and watch. There's no machine for you. I've too many pilots as it is.'

That seemed to me the last straw. I hid in my cabin until it was time for dinner. *Que diable allais-je faire dans cette galère?* That was the right name for this vessel—a galley. What on earth had I been sent here for?

III

At dinner that night there was some effort at conversation, but it was not sustained. Almost everyone seemed afflicted with unnatural reserve. Alone the two flight-commanders spoke with any freedom, seated one on either side of an empty chair in which, I supposed, the squadron-commander would presently take his place. Only one other pilot spoke much above a whisper and he was a man who had recently been awarded a Military Cross for bringing down a German machine. He was not much older than I, very little senior in the Flying Corps; I would have liked to talk with him, to listen to his account of the fight. But he was very sullen, with a perpetual scowl on his face emphasised by a peak of hair growing low over his forehead almost to the bridge of his nose. He spoke only to the senior flight-commander, who gave him a patronising smile every now and then.

Half-way through the meal, the squadron-commander entered and made for the empty chair, murmuring faintly, 'Don't get up, don't get up,' as everyone rose to his feet. When all were seated again, Growl, my flight-commander, suddenly remembered me and I had to walk round the table to shake hands while the entire company stared in open-mouthed silence as though I were some newly discovered disease. The major gave me a limp hand together with a tired smile, and if I had not been so nervous myself I should have seen at once that, amongst other things, he was cursed with shyness. After I had returned to my place dead silence reigned which he attempted to break by speaking to everyone in turn. But it was always with that same tired smile, in a quiet, rather nasal voice, his eyes half-veiled like a coy maiden's, ready to turn hastily away from embarrassing talkativeness. He seemed satisfied at rarely eliciting anything more than a 'Yes, sir,' or 'No, Sir,' by way of response. Conversation dwindled gradually to a sort of timid squeaking of mice in the wainscot when the cat is near. It was plain that he was not popular in the squadron.

And yet he was in many ways a good man. In the long run I came to esteem him as much as any member of that peculiar squadron. But he was too reserved and aloof from his juniors. He had been a gunner before the war, and what in those palmy days had persuaded him to exchange the dignified security of his regiment for the risky unconventionality of the Flying Corps is more than I shall ever know. Perhaps, being like most gunners brainy and fond of maths, he thought to find those attributes useful in the air. But he was not a good pilot, seldom flew, and had none of that fire which I then believed and later knew to be essential in the leader of a good squadron. Nevertheless my heart warmed to him when one day, in the course of a rare conversation, he confided to me that he thought Surtees in some ways superior to Dickens.

Naturally upon the evening of my arrival I knew nothing of all this; yet I did receive a first and definite impression not so much of him alone as of all the men sitting about the gloomy table. They were bored. Bored with one another, bored with the war, bored even with flying. And the boredom seemed to be working from the head down to the feet. I don't go so far as to suggest that the major himself was bored with his command, but whatever enthusiasm he may have felt was stifled by his own reserve. The flight-commanders could hardly be inspired by his leadership, and the junior pilots had little or no incentive to strike out on their own. Joy was not the only thing lacking. The very life seemed, to my first ignorant glance, to be ebbing from the mess in the barge as though we were the doomed crew of a derelict ship.

Towards the end of dinner my neighbour at the table jogged my elbow.

'Pass the bread, please,' he said in a hoarse whisper.

I had been spoken to.

IV

When we had risen from table I went up alone on deck and made my way to the bows of the barge. It was a gloriously fine night, starlit, windless and warm. Leaning my arms upon the rail, I looked down over the side. Upon the towpath along the opposite bank a man and a girl strolled, arms about each other's shoulders linking them so closely that in the dusk they seemed to be one very broad person with two voices. The man talked in low tones; at every pause the girl's laughter rang out clearly. As they came abreast of where I stood, there was a scurrying in the bank beneath them, the plop of a small body falling into the water, and the darkly shining surface of the river showed for a moment the arrowhead wash of a water-rat. There were few flowers nearby, but from the farm came a blend of warm, homely odours, of cattle and of straw. Close at hand it was very peaceful.

I leaned back against a deck-house, raising my eyes to the tall poplars sweeping the sky. Beyond them to the east the horizon flickered with intermittent fire, alternating from orange-yellow to greenish white. An incessant racket shook the air. Every few seconds calcium flares rocketed to the heavens, hesitated, then parachuted slowly earthwards, silhouetting the poplars and rimming their leaves with frozen light as though with hoar-frost. For an instant the countryside would be silent beneath the garish light, the trees motionless as if afraid, and then as darkness fell again distant machine-guns clattered anxiously at some unseen foe. Ragged bursts of rifle fire broke out suddenly like the angry barking of a disturbed pack of hounds. A shell sighed heavily over, settled down wearily; its explosion silenced the barking as if a door had been slammed in the kennels. Far to the south countless guns drummed with monotonous insistence the prelude to the battle of Loos.

From where I stood the nearest point of the firing line was under four miles distant. The noise made it seem even less, and yet viewed from the peaceful countryside it did not seem like war. Without stretching the imagination I could fancy myself watching the grand finale of fireworks at a big local fair. The surprising thing was that I should be watching alone. The only two possible spectators in the vicinity, the man and the girl on the towpath, were heedless of both the menacing gunfire and the display of coloured lights. It was as though they had tired of the noise and grim fun of that fair to the east and had sought the solitude of the river-bank to do their courting in the dark shadow of the poplars. They did not see me and I turned away from them to gaze at the unintended beauty of the battle scene.

All at once, from some room beneath my feet, a gramophone blared. It played the Foxtrot, latest of London dances; but its screeching was like an insult; a mockery of the night's tragedy. A voice from a cabin near the stern yelled furiously: 'Stop that bloody row!' The squeaky record came to an abrupt stop. A mile away a heavy shell burst impressively. . . .

When I went below to the mess the senior flight-commander and his sulky friend with the Military Cross were drinking whisky together, in silence and without any apparent enjoyment. Another couple were playing chess. All four looked up in surprise at my muttered 'Good night.'

V

I had dreaded the morning and its threat of further encounters with the silent members of the squadron, its lack of anything to do except, as Growl had put it, to 'hang around'. But I was immensely cheered when after breakfast I was ordered to jump into a Crossley about to leave for St Omer. At the headquarters aerodrome, it appeared, I should find an aeroplane waiting to be flown back to the squadron. . . . For the organisation which wasted two days and two cars on moving one small pilot I was deeply grateful, since had I been told on the previous day to fly direct to the squadron I should never have found it even with the most accurate of maps. As for landing, I would certainly have crashed had I not been able to walk over the ground first to note the position of treacherous ditches and rough ground.

The drive itself was pleasant enough, but, as I might have expected, when I reached the aerodrome it was to discover that nothing was known of any aeroplane to be delivered to the squadron. In an office hut a polite but argumentative young man informed me that he had plenty of aeroplanes to dispose of—at a price. The price being a paper of written instructions, an official document or a signed order of some sort—a bond, in fact, by way of payment. I had nothing except my own word and Growl's command which I repeated but which did not seem to carry much weight. We spent all the morning and part of the afternoon haggling, as it might have been over the price of a rug in an Oriental *souk*. At length when the young man saw that he could not get rid of me because I did not know where else to go, he took pity and ordered an aeroplane to be brought from the sheds.

The machine was only a Shorthorn and not very smart at that, but to me she was more precious than gold. She was to be my own aeroplane, the machine in which I was, to all intents and purposes, going to win the war single-handed —that is, if ever I managed to get her safely back to the squadron. I inspected her with the utmost care, examined her log-books, warmed up her engine slowly; too slowly for the attendant mechanics, as soon as I was settled in the *nacelle* they whisked away the wheel chocks and departed. I was left alone with my machine. No one took any further interest; St Omer aerodrome was deserted. I took off unnoticed.

In contrast to the previous day the weather had turned cold and damp; the wind was against me and there were banks of cloud below two thousand feet. I flew beneath them, anxious not to miss the aerodrome. The Forêt de Nieppe was a sure guide to the neighbourhood and after that the River Lys, but it was necessary to be cautious. Flanders is a patchwork quilt from the air, and the aerodrome lay close to the lines. I found it at last, the smallest of all the surrounding fields, and when I had landed and taxied the Shorthorn up to the hangars by the riverside I felt that a good day's work had been done.

Even Growl deigned to unbend a little. He exclaimed tersely that he was glad I had not crashed. Profiting from this favourable reception I asked if I could do a job of work on the morrow; I was keen to start, there were important operations afoot. Perhaps he was a little embarrassed by my persistence, or else he was suffering from remorse after his first unnecessarily severe treatment of me (for now I was flinging salutes at him upon the slightest provocation); at any rate after staring in silence for a few moments he told me grumpily that I could take the Shorthorn up in the morning. An experienced observer would be sent with me to show me the lines and to see that I did not get lost. I saluted again, but I could have jumped for joy.

VI

The members of the mess were rather more lively at dinner that night. The great attack at Loos was in full blast; rumours of success were current. The squadron had done much good work during the day, mainly artillery observation; even the major showed that he was pleased by loosening up a little. At the end of the meal he sent the mess-servants out of the room, had the doors carefully closed and read us the latest official *communiqués*, together with a vaguely humorous Intelligence Report generally known as 'Comic Cuts'. At the time it was thrilling to listen to the reading of events that might be more decisive than any since Waterloo.

It appeared that our infantry had overrun the enemy trench system, taking huge numbers of prisoners and guns. A break-through had almost been achieved, was expected within twenty-four hours. The cavalry were ready! Far away to the south the French had attacked on an even larger scale in Champagne, a wide sector of the German line had been pierced, cavalry were beginning to advance. The enemy, demoralised at the two simultaneous offensives, would probably retire all along the front to avoid being caught in the pincer-like concentration of the victorious Allies. . . . And so on and so forth.

The duties of the Royal Flying Corps were announced in a secret document accompanied by a very secret map. The map was handed round to be seen and initialled by each officer. It showed the general scheme of the forthcoming campaign, the points to be attacked after the success of the first blow at Loos. The time and date of each further advance were marked, the distances of the objectives growing once the trench lines had been passed. And after the trenches —open warfare! Red lines and arrows showed the roads by which our transport would advance. The red lines ran eastward for miles before meeting a vertical black stroke south of Lille, representing the first position at which the enemy might hope to make a stand against our terrific onslaught. Thence dotted red lines with smaller arrows, dates with question marks in brackets showed that the great advance was to be pressed still farther. The roads to Brussels were shown. 'Brussels by Christmas,' it was said.

VII

It was so bright and sunny in the morning that, with victory flying on the wings of rumour, I would have been
very unhappy had I been condemned to stay on the ground.
But Growl was as good as his word. The Shorthorn was
ready at the appointed hour; waiting near her I found the
observer who was to accompany me. We took off from the
aerodrome without delay.

Guided by the observer, I began by steering a northerly
course, following the Lys towards Armentières. The map
was consulted frequently so that I should get to know the few
outstanding landmarks, but aside from the river itself and
the distant hill of Cassel there was little enough of importance or interest. Innumerable strips of cultivated land made
a good natural camouflage, rendering observation difficult.
I saw a man and two horses ploughing, a farm cart being
driven down a narrow track, a toy train puffing along a
thread-like railway. But there were no large-scale movements
and, save to the east, no signs of war. The Lys, winding like
a snake, made me think of d'Artagnan and Milady. . . .

We reached Armentières and started to turn. The town
had been a good deal knocked about by gunfire, the streets
were deserted; but the railway station, or a portion of it,
was evidently in use. Close by were an engine with steam
up and a large number of trucks. Eastwards the double
track ran straight towards Lille; it was pockmarked with
shell-holes, overgrown with weeds. My eyes followed it over
the nose of the machine as we turned. There was a point
where the railway lines and their beds were cut by a trench;
a short, uninterrupted stretch of rails, and then another
trench. The shell-holes were more numerous. I was above
the firing line.

Turning south, I stared down intently at the battle-front.
And my first impression was of its immensity. It was in-
credibly vast. It did not seem possible that men had made all
this mess within one short year. From the North Sea to
the Alps! But surely there must be some other way in which
the war could be waged. Loos? Ah, yes, that was the way
to do it. It was strangely exciting to think that in the south
we were actually breaking through the whole system, that

we should soon be out in the open again, guns limbering up and galloping forward, cavalry reconnoitring and charging, infantry marching along dusty roads, deploying in fresh country, taking cover to fire from hedges instead of from holes in the ground. Scarcely worth my while to 'learn' this old trench-line so carefully; we should soon be flying east.

It was while my attention was concentrated upon the ground, where I was trying to locate a village shown upon the map but which seemed to have been obliterated in the extraordinary welter of digging, that I received a nerve-racking shock. Something—much more than the worst air bump I had ever felt—struck the machine. She quivered and vibrated violently. I started in alarm, uncertain whether the engine was breaking up or if something even more serious had befallen. Momentarily I was afraid that one of the wings had snapped off—a thought which frequently came to me in a Shorthorn. But over my shoulder I could see nothing unusual, the wings were in place, the propeller revolved, the alarm-clocks ticked. . . . Again the machine shook, seemed to hesitate in her flight, rocked uncontrollably. Fear swung my head round; beyond the wing tip I saw blue-grey vapour drifting by. Fire? The paralysing thought had scarcely come into my head before a third jolt, greater than the first two put together, almost unseated me. Like an explosion—and it came from beneath my feet, jarring the floor of the *nacelle* as though some unseen giant had kicked it. I turned to look forward, mystified as much as scared. And there in front of the machine's nose I saw unrolling, like a ball of soft wool, a puff of yellowish smoke. I looked back; astern were two more puffs, already less dense, dissipating slowly. I was being shelled.

The likelihood of such an occurrence was something I had entirely forgotten. Growl had said nothing to me about anti-aircraft fire, but then he had not expected me to be so foolish as to sit passively over the German lines on my first visit to them. And for an opening salvo the shooting seemed dangerously accurate; I felt uncomfortable even now that the surprise was past. Furiously I trod upon the harmonium pedals, waggling the bespectacled handlebars as nervously as on my first solo. A tap on the shoulder made me twist my head in renewed alarm.

'It's all right,' the observer yelled in my ear. 'Better turn away from the lines.'

The shelling went on, but the machine shook less after each explosion, until only a slight air-bump lifted one wing or the other some time after a shell had burst. Eventually the firing became an entertainment at which I could afford to smile, a harmless spectacle like that I had witnessed from the deck of the barge. A few minutes later, steadying the machine on a southerly course, I looked back to the east. Three, six, nine—a dozen fading puffs dotted the sky. More than a dozen high-explosive shells at one inoffensive Shorthorn and no damage done! It seemed too much. A waste of valuable ammunition, and therefore well worth the trouble of being fired at if only to annoy the enemy and make him wear out his guns.

The thought warmed me. I wanted more of the entertainment, also I wanted to get used to it without getting hurt. When at length the firing ceased altogether, to have turned away did not strike me as being a very noble action. I was already some three miles from the front lines whence I had departed at nearly sixty miles an hour. I felt rather ashamed. And of a sudden a silly feeling of bravado came over me. Without consulting the observer, I banked and steered due east.

The intricate diggings of the British passed underneath the *nacelle*. No movement was to be seen anywhere. Across No Man's Land the inside of the enemy trenches became distinct. The positions appeared to be unoccupied. Not a sign of life nor of death; not a sound audible above the clatter of the engine, not a shell burst upon the invaders' front. Hard to believe that even one man was alive down there; none at least to take notice of me.

The machine travelled steadily east; the enemy lines began to thin out. Soon I was over open country in occupied territory. I had, so to speak, thrown down the gauntlet—although Heaven preserve me from throwing out even a glove with a wooden propeller behind my head!—and I had disobeyed orders. That seemed to be enough for one morning's work. Not a solitary German to be seen either on the ground or in the sky, and the anti-aircraft gunners had apparently gone off to lunch. It was becoming rather dull.

And then it came down like a hailstorm—or rather it came up. There were a couple of explosions as though lightning had struck close to my head, and a moment later the whole sky crackled into life. On either side and straight in front were yellow flashes; black walls of angry-looking smoke unrolled themselves from nothing like a conjuring trick. I could see pieces of metal flying through the air that had become as rough as a choppy sea in a tideway. It did not seem credible that all this stuff could be coming up from the quiet earth, but more as if a host of malignant spirits had materialised in mid-air. It made me accomplish the quickest about-turn I had so far attempted in an aeroplane. With the throttle hard open and the nose pushed well down, I fled westwards.

The air-speed rose to sixty-five. Things shook and vibrated, the engine rattled, the wind whistled in the wires. Over my shoulder I saw the observer, his jaw set, clinging rigidly to the sides of the *nacelle*. But we got through the storm. The bursting shells became less frequent, less startlingly loud as No Man's Land was left behind. The silent British lines received us into their quiet atmosphere. And the enemy's last shot sounded no more harmful than a husky, deprecating cough.

Pulling out the map, I laid off a straight course for home. Far ahead the shining water of the Lys winked through a familiar row of poplars.

After a successful landing I got out and looked under the wings of the Shorthorn to see what scars she might bear of the tremendous bombardment to which she had been subjected. For a long time I hunted high and low. I was disappointed. Near one of the wing tips I discovered two small holes. . . .

In the afternoon we read headlines in an English daily paper: '*Two Real Victories At Last!*' Champagne and Loos —September, 1915. 'At last'—it sounded more like a sigh of relief than a cry of triumph. 'Real?'—by nightfall we learned that the attacks had been held up.

VIII

'You had your first look at the lines today, didn't you?'
a young pilot asked me at dinner. I stared dumbly, unable
to credit the fact that I was being spoken to in a normal
tone of voice. When the truth had sunk in I nodded, still
unable to find my tongue. He went on in a manner of polite
enquiry, smiling a little. 'How did you like it?'

I pulled myself together, forced an answer and mentioned
that there had been a certain amount of 'Archie' (the name
invariably used for anti-aircraft fire and derived from a
pre-war comic song: '*Archibald—certainly not!*'). From the
other side of the table Growl looked up quickly.

'What? You were "Archied"? You must have been damn'
scared, weren't you?'

I admitted that I had been very scared; but I added
that, once I got used to it, it had not seemed so terrible
after all. I imagined that it could never be so unpleasant
as heavy shelling on the ground.

This, the longest speech I had yet made in the squadron,
was greeted with a look of severe displeasure from Growl.
His tone in reply was as nasty as any he had yet used to me.

'Don't talk nonsense!' he said cuttingly. 'Just wait, young
fellow, until you've had a bit more experience before you
talk lightly about Archie.'

From farther down the table the other flight-commander
blinked, as though he were seeing me for the first time and
did not much appreciate what he saw. He had thin, rather
demure lips, sly red-rimmed eyes and a long nose. He
looked something like a fair-haired fox.

'Who says he doesn't mind Archie?' he demanded staring at me. 'Good God, just because you've seen a couple
of shells in the distance you think you know a lot, don't
you? The first time you really get fired at you'll go all "goosey"
and try to run like a hare. Hot air that's what you're suffering
from!'

At the end he suddenly smiled at me in quite a friendly
fashion as if implying that we had now been introduced.
The Military Cross pilot by his side laughed silently, looking down at his soup as though anxious to avoid my gaze
and pretended that he was not laughing at me. I had nothing

to say in answer, for I was quite ready to admit that I knew less than anyone in the world about aerial warfare. But I could not fathom the reasons for so much fierceness. Could it be that Archie was really so fearsome, or were they trying to scare me? If so, why?

After dinner I stayed on for some time talking to the friendly young pilot beside me and thus I learned the names of the others, also some belated information about the squadron and its work. The members of the third Flight, I heard, lived 'ashore' in a farmhouse half a mile away. They messed separately and were in other ways almost independent of the squadron. They had a flight-commander who was, it appeared, a wonderful man, exceptionally good at artillery observation, experienced at bombing and photography, keen on fighting in the air and a jolly good fellow to boot. From the way he was described to me I pictured him as someone midway between Napoleon and God. He was obviously too good for this squadron and I was not surprised to hear that he was soon leaving it to command one of his own.

My new friend was known as 'Wilhelm', or 'Little Willie', because he bore a faint facial resemblance to the war-time caricature of the German Crown Prince. He was never allowed to forget the fact, but he took his daily dose of chaff in good part.

Presently we found ourselves listening to the conversation of the only two remaining men in the mess, the foxy flight-commander and his Military Cross friend. 'Foxy' could be very funny at times, but his sense of humour was of a sort that wisdom should have counselled him to hide. He had a perpetual if comical sneer for everything and everyone. He scoffed at the major, derided Growl, laughed at pilots who had met with misfortune in peace or war, and ridiculed the better known members of the Flying Corps in France. The conversation ran something like this:

MILITARY CROSS (politely and in a low voice): What has become of that fellow —— who used to fly at Hendon before the war?

FOXY (vehemently): That damn' fool? Why, he crashed months ago in England and was completely *carboneezay*—tee-hee!

M.C. (laughing): *What* was that word?

FOXY: *Carboneezay?* That's what the French papers always say when a fellow is burnt to death, it means carbonised. Before the war it was the usual thing in France, after every flight. The papers just put in a paragraph saying: 'Mr Smith took his machine up last week. He was *complètemong carboneezay;* his widow looks very pretty in black.' Tee-hee-hee!

Not knowing the late pilot personally I ventured a mild laugh which drew from Foxy a smile of gratification, but from M.C. a scowl of annoyance. It was plain that the direct way to Foxy's heart was to laugh at his jokes; that, however, was something M.C. regarded as his privilege and monopoly. I noticed that he went on hurriedly to other topics so as to prevent the conversation from becoming general.

'I wonder what has happened to young G——?' he asked Foxy. G—— was a pilot who had been missing from the squadron for a day or two, having failed to return from a reconnaissance.*

'Oh, he's all right,' Foxy replied cheerfully. 'He has "gone west" sure enough. He's probably having the time of his life dining with the Kaiser in Potsdam!'

At this sally M.C. was unable to contain his mirth and choked, red in the face. Foxy smilingly patted him on the back and ordered a round of drinks. Conversation came gradually back again to the subject of G——.

'He *was* a silly young lad,' Foxy went on. 'What the devil did he want to go so far over the lines for? He had rotten weather as an excuse for not going at all. But it's the major's fault really, he could easily have handed the job on to another squadron. Still, young G—— ought to have had the sense to back out. That's the worst of a lot of the pilots in this squadron, they're so beastly keen to go chasing over the lines—think they're going to get covered with honour and glory, I suppose. And all they achieve is either to get shot down and *carboneezay* or join the Kaiser for a meal in Potsdam. Makes me go all "goosey" to think of it!'

M.C. was still chuckling as I left.

* Some days later we heard that he had been killed and his observer taken prisoner.

IX

After another preliminary flight to study the topography of the trenches and the country from Armentières to Lens, I began to follow a regular routine of patrolling the lines, generally at dawn, on the watch for enemy aircraft. The other Shorthorns of the Flight had similar work to do at different periods of the day, while the remaining Flights now re-equipped with the new B.E.2c.s performed the more important tasks of reconnaissance and artillery observation. The B.E. pilots got most of the hard knocks and, therefore, most of the credit.

Patrolling was dull work to pilots of greater experience provided with more efficient machines, but for me those early morning flights never lost their thrill, nor the spice of adventure its flavour. Flying itself was always interesting, apart from the war, even if you had to do it in a staid old Shorthorn; and although for a long time very few German aeroplanes were visible on our sector of the front there were plenty of sideshows to keep one wide awake. There were anti-aircraft batteries to spot and report so that they might be dealt with by our own guns, enemy artillery positions to be noted and any change reported, unusual movements in the trenches (such as saps being pushed forward) to be observed. Since the patrol took place above the lines careful observation would also reveal activity of troops or transport in the areas immediately behind the front. And although much of this was of minor importance, a good observer would as a rule bring back a list of small facts useful in compiling the Intelligence Report.

But the fact remained that the principal object of these defensive patrols was to prevent German aircraft from crossing the lines to reconnoitre, bomb or take photographs. On our section of the front there was not, after the failure of the Loos battle, much activity of any sort, in the air practically none. German aeroplanes did come over the front occasionally, but it was not their policy, as it was ours, to carry out numerous daily offensive flights. In the air they were on the defensive whereas the Flying Corps believed in maintaining as many machines as possible over the enemy's territory. Whether this policy of ours was wholly wise or

Dawn on the Lys. *Sketch by the author*

Remains of 4086. German photograph of the author's B.E.2c, identified from the official records by the serial number on the fin

not is a matter of opinion; it was certainly in keeping with the spirit of the majority of our pilots; but there can be no doubt that we lost many more machines than the Germans and that engine failure—a fairly common thing—cost us many prisoners. From my personal point of view the safer policy of the enemy made patrolling the front very uneventful.

The heavens are immense and a Shorthorn slow; even admitting that the sky, within an aeroplane's range of action, is not limitless it is big enough to restrict the utility of a low-powered craft. From two thousand feet, the lowest height at which an enemy would be likely to come over, up to ten thousand, which was the Shorthorn's ceiling, along a front of twenty miles was a vast area. If at the northern end of the beat one sighted a suspicious aircraft to the south—a mere dot in the sky—it was all very well opening the throttle wide and pushing the machine's nose down in pursuit; unless the two aeroplanes happened to be travelling towards each other, the twain, like East and West, would assuredly never meet. The Shorthorn having less speed than most British and far less than any German aeroplane, could not hope to overtake. Pursuit from any distance was such a hopeless business that the best course open to us was to cruise up and down the front, trying to look important so as to scare away German machines, making meanwhile all possible observations of the ground on the enemy's side. Then at the end of each flight we would generally descend to within a thousand feet or so of the lines for the observer to practise with his Lewis gun and teach the enemy in the trenches to keep their heads down.

X

Early in October I attacked an enemy kite-balloon. I note the occurrence because it was my first experience of an aerial engagement, and not because the performance was either remarkable or very successful.

The patrol started just after dawn that day. The morning was dark, cloudy, strips of angry orange light to the east emphasised the sombre aspect of the battle scene. There was no wind and a heavy dew made the fabric droop slackly

c

over the planes of the Shorthorn. There was an autumn dampness in the cool air; I was inclined to think that there was very little 'lift' in it.

But we took off easily enough; the clattering of the engine smashed the quiet of the new day while the propeller's draught bent the poplars as we sailed narrowly over them. Upon the deck of the barge Growl stood gazing upwards. I imagined his feelings: relief at seeing me off so punctually, gruff ill-humour at being disturbed from his slumbers. It was a joy to be in the air. I headed for Armentières.

As usual there was nothing much doing in the northern part of our sector. Most of the activity was confined to the areas from La Bassée to Lens where the aftermath of the Loos battle still dragged on—desultory but fierce fighting for the possession of broken trenches and disputed shell-holes, local attacks and counter-attacks about mounds exalted in this flat country to the war-time importance of 'hills'. The quiet line to the north had to be watched, naturally, but if the Shorthorn was ever to score any points worth the marking it was to the south that her efforts would have to be concentrated.

From Armentières I turned to follow a zig-zag course over Fleurbaix, Laventie, Neuve-Chapelle, and Festubert. All along this stretch the trenches lay silent, clearly defined, almost respectable in their tidiness. But south of La Bassée a thin yellow fog hung ominously over the chaos of devastated land as though to hide its shame from the watchful heavens. Smoke rose from burning ruins, through the haze the flashes of guns flickered balefully, puffs of smoke and dust rose from the chalky soil. It was an evil sight, yet since it was also the scene of the tragedy which held our hopes and our hearts, there was something in it that stirred a desire to share in the adventure.

A mile inside the German lines at a height of five thousand feet there floated something like an elephant's appendix much inflamed. On calm sunny days, from a safe distance behind the front, I have seen observation balloons looking graceful, creamy yellow, bright with the red, white and blue circles of our national markings, toy-like with the little *nacelle* dangling and the string holding it, one must suppose, to some excited lad playing in a field below. But on this day, above a grim battlefield there was no charm or beauty in that sinister German intestine. Rather it seemed to be the genius presiding over the evil deeds of men on the ground, the eye searching for blood. I took a sudden dislike to that balloon, it disgraced the morning sky. It was grey-green with a black cross upon its ugly side. It must be destroyed or at least made to go down. I banked and pointed the Shorthorn viciously at it.

Many people used to think that a balloon was a harmless sort of thing, unable to defend itself, but nothing was harmless against a Shorthorn. And although the balloon itself was not armed it had powerful allies on earth; at least one battery of anti-aircraft guns near its mooring place, another a short distance away. For aeroplanes that ventured to descend below two or three thousand feet there were groups of machine-guns to be reckoned with and, since the attendants of these weapons had nothing to do but to watch the balloon whose height they already knew, when an aeroplane began the attack they all let fly. Sometimes a long line of observation balloons might, owing to the scarcity of guns and to the very length of the line, be less efficiently guarded; a single balloon had the attention of the whole neighbourhood.

As we hastened—I use the word with care, in relation to a Shorthorn—towards the balloon there came a scattered volley of Archie shells. The bursts were very unevenly spaced, some of them so far off that I could barely hear their apologetic coughing. I pointed to the balloon, yelling back at the observer when and where he was to open fire. He had the machine-gun, a Lewis, and he had to be careful how he used it. In the Shorthorn there was only the most primitive form of gun-mounting which limited the field of fire to a very small arc. He could not fire straight ahead because I was in the way, and he could not fire astern or indeed anywhere abaft the beam because of the engine, the propeller and the forest of struts braced with piano-wire. Only on either bow could he get a clear shot.

I put the balloon on my port bow and dived towards it. (A dive which in these days would be considered a flat glide.) The engine rattled and shook; the air-speed indicator showed nearly seventy, which was, I think, about as much as this particular craft could stand. The balloon came rapidly nearer. But so did the Archie shells. Their explosions now contained an unpleasantly sharp menace; once or twice I heard a sudden click and thud as when a penny is pushed into a slot-machine: the wings were being hit. We were still between two and three hundred yards from the balloon when I waved my arm for the observer to open fire.

The loud clatter of the machine-gun close to my left ear was rather inspiring. At last, I thought, we are engaging an aerial target, an enemy! But the effect was disappointing. With memories, I suppose, of toy balloons, I had expected this one to go pop at the first prick of a bullet's impact; now with growing annoyance I realised that the low pressure in the bag would only let the gas escape by slow degrees. We could do no more than puncture it; we could not even set it on fire for we had no special incendiary ammunition. Short of flying so close as to be able to dig our teeth into it, there were no means of destroying the hateful· thing. It was infuriating. Here we were in a powerful (*sic*) aeroplane, armed with a deadly machine-gun, yet we could do nothing to a mere sausage.

And then I noticed something very odd. I had brought the Shorthorn quite near to the balloon, so that Archie, for fear of hitting his own side, was easing off, and having banked the machine to port I was circling round to give the observer the best chance of firing. He had put in several bursts, unable to miss so big a target, when I found that I was being compelled to push the nose further and further down in order to keep the balloon in the same favourable position. The truth only gradually penetrated my mind. The balloon was being hauled in.

The observer had finished a drum of ammunition, the balloon was going down fast, and Archie was becoming troublesome. We had done all that we could for the time being. I turned back to the lines. In less than a minute we had crossed them and Archie faded away. Much relieved, I throttled down the engine to give it a rest.

Looking astern I could not find the balloon where I expected it to be. I searched the sky, or as much of it as I could see, but no balloon. Had we then, by some fortunate chance, destroyed it utterly? Banking the machine, I stared down—then up. . . . It was still there, large as life and actually higher than before! Turning the machine about, swiftly I headed back to the east, balloon-murder in my heart.

It was above us at the start, I wondered whether we should be able to climb steeply enough if they went on letting out the string. But as soon as they saw us coming they began pulling it in, evidently anxious to have no more trouble. It did not go down very fast and was at about our own level when we came within reasonably close range. This time I made directly for it, the observer pointing the gun from close beside my head.

At the very instant when he opened fire, Archie came crashing up with renewed energy and fair accuracy. I began wishing myself somewhere else. The situation was distinctly alarming because I was once more a long way over the lines, heading for Germany at under three thousand feet; if the engine were hit I might not be able to get home. . . . The balloon was going down faster now, faster than I could follow without risking trouble with the Shorthorn. At two thousand feet I levelled off and the observer ceased fire. For a moment I thought of going still lower to start again, but as I throttled down to glide there came to me above the rush of wind, the sound of fire from the ground, the faint *crack-crack* of passing bullets from well-aimed rifle fire. It was plain that things were getting much too hot; opening wide the throttle I turned homewards. The balloon was well down and I felt convinced that we had made it leak sufficiently to keep it on the ground for a day or two. But I no longer cared much, for I was not sure if we should get back safely.

There were moments as I zig-zagged towards the English trenches, which, for all their devastation, now seemed peaceful and friendly, there were moments when I was sure the flight would end in disaster. Archie was continuous, close and fierce. One shell sent a multitude of fragments to rattle a sonata upon the piano-wires, two of which snapped. If many more of them went, then according to all the rules the wings would fall off. I made another wild zig-zag, only to bring us closer to a shell whose wide flash glowed angrily through the smoke. I saw a large fragment fly past. There was a crash behind me, and twisting round I saw that in the top plane, immediately above the observer, a hole had

opened as big as your fist. Banking in the opposite direction
I drove the nose down for increased speed, my only
remedy. . . .

But the worst was over. In a short time Archie lost the
range and the shell explosions dwindled again to harmless
coughs. A few seconds more and we were well over the
British lines where the battle seemed to have stopped—'to
watch us', I supposed proudly in my joy at being safe.

Turning to the north-west, reducing speed and following
the front at a respectful distance, we finished the patrol.
We were out of ammunition, almost out of fuel. Now for
breakfast. Presently the River Lys and a tall line of poplars
came in sight. From three thousand feet I began a slow
straight glide, mindful of the advice that it is not wise to
stunt an aeroplane after she has been fired at.

Before landing I took a long look back to the east. Clouds
there were, and autumn haze, and fading Archie puffs. But
no longer were the heavens marred by a German kite-
balloon.

XI

'So you attacked a sausage and forced him down, did
you?' Growl's voice, still gruff and fierce, was softer than
I had ever heard it. He was pleased, and that was something
I had almost ceased to hope for. My observer having left
the sheds first had evidently given him some of the details.
I went on to explain more fully what we had done. Growl's
face darkened.

'To get as close as that you must have been a long way
over the lines,' he grumbled.

I explained hastily.

'Not so very far. You see, the balloon was quite near the
front and . . .'

'Nonsense!' he interrupted. 'I've seen that balloon myself
and it's a long way back. I thought you had orders not to
cross the lines? You're looking for trouble, young fellow-
me-lad!'

I tried to protest that I had taken no unnecessary risks,
that the sausage had tempted me. Growl turned his back

and disappeared down the barge's companion ladder.

Later in the morning I encountered the major. He smiled distantly at the vibrating salute I gave in an attempt to mollify the wrath to come, and then murmured something about a 'good show—under heavy fire—machine quite badly hit'. And without another word he strolled off, looking about him and moving his thin sandy-coloured head like a melancholy bird. A lonely, austere figure, I thought him.

In the mess I was wise enough to hold my tongue. Any remarks on the subject of my morning's adventure would, I felt sure, be greeted with biting sarcasm by the more senior pilots. Alone to Wilhelm, who had been the first to converse with me and with whom I was fast becoming acquainted, did I announce the facts of the affair. I spoke quietly so as not to draw attention to myself, but I could see by the glance I got from M.C. and the sidelong look of suspicion from Foxy that the less I said the better. It was something approaching impertinence for a Shorthorn pilot to attempt a combat in the air.

The real trouble with me in this squadron was that I did not in the least understand the others. If I did anything good they seemed to regard it as impudence, if I did nothing they did not speak to me or so much as acknowledge my existence. It would, I think, have pleased them most had I been sent away in disgrace. That would have given them something to talk about.

One of the pilots had developed piles. He was very shy and ashamed about it himself. But it became the standing joke of the squadron. Everyone sniggered whenever he came near, and coarse innuendoes were continually made in his hearing. My own troubles seemed much smaller by com-parison. I was glad that I had not got piles.

XII

Days of bad weather followed, during which scarcely any work could be done in the air, and a great deal of ping-pong was played in the mess; then the Shorthorn, her wounds patched and repaired, was up again on patrol. Upon alternate days I was on duty in the afternoon, watching the line during the hours of artillery spotting. But it was less interesting then than in the early mornings; what activity there might have been seemed always to have died down after lunch. The line was quiet, the sky deserted.

One day in search of enemy aircraft I went up through a ragged bank of clouds, climbing persistently until we came out in glorious sunshine above a limitless white plain of motionless, frozen mountains. 'Another world'—how often that has been said of the space above the clouds, when the earth is hidden and one is alone with the sun and the wind. It is more than a mere expression; it is indeed the first stage of that journey to the stars. . . .

An hour's steady climbing brought the Shorthorn to over ten thousand feet (the aneroid showed eleven thousand eight hundred). It was the highest I had yet been in the air and, beyond that the machine resolutely refused to go. I looked around to see what advantage might be drawn from this great altitude. To the east I caught sight of a black speck. Was it one of our machines on reconnaissance or an enemy? Probably the latter, but I was unable to find out for certain, since although I turned towards it at once to investigate I could get no closer. The speck maintained its distance, heading north. At this height the Shorthorn's air-speed was down to well under fifty, and I had difficulty in keeping her level; the nose had a tendency to sink earthwards. To seek a fight under such conditions was worse than useless; it was asking for trouble.

Giving up the attempt to close the suspected enemy I throttled down, and with only the wind in the wires and a soft ticking from the engine we sailed down through the clouds into the mists of the war zone. Over the enemy lines we went low to fire a few score rounds into their trenches, while Archie flashed sporadically but did no damage. The Shorthorn was not easy to control in really bumpy weather; in the disturbed air beneath the clouds we rolled and pitched uncomfortably on the way home.

Next day we were out on patrol again, but not then nor on succeeding flights could I get her to fly so high. She was getting tired.

XIII

The days of the Shorthorn were numbered. A regular supply of the new aeroplanes was now available; machines of the older type were being sent back to the depot. Eventually there were only two left in the squadron. Mine was the last to go.

A few patrol flights, mostly uneventful, and then warned for a practice flight on a B.E. I was forced to desert the Shorthorn for good. Poor old lady, she was too slow and antiquated to be of any further use. She could never hope to catch up with an enemy, or fight him successfully if she herself were caught up. On artillery observation she was an easy prey for Archie or a German scout, and it was hard to understand why, on patrol, I had so long been left unmolested. During those short but frequent crossings of the lines any of the newer opposing machines could, in spite of my hopeful optimism, have had her entirely at their mercy. But perhaps the German aviators did not think it worth their while, or did they respect the dignity of her age?

I took her off the ground for the last time with a feeling of sorrow. She had served her purpose, she had worked nobly; she had proved herself reliable, trustworthy, incapable of vicious or underhand tricks. She bore the marks of her patience under fire, her endurance was witnessed by honourable scars: a dozen patches on her white wings, new wires here and there, a bound strut, a patch of darker paint on her *nacelle*.

She was, in a sense, too much of a lady, not 'fast' enough to be efficient for the demands of an increasingly sophisticated war; and, since for training purposes there were plenty of her kind in England, she herself was to be taken away and dismantled, reduced to her component parts. A few, a very few of those parts might eventually find their way as useful scrap to some aircraft factory, but as an individual her life was finished, her identity destroyed when her number was erased from the books. Yet to me she will remain as I used so often to see her in the uncertain light of daybreak. In memory I can see her still, from the deck of the barge where half-dressed I have come to sip hastily from a steaming-hot cup of tea. She stands before her canvas hangar, her large

yet frail-looking wings outspread, glistening with dew. Her
nacelle points towards the east whence come the stealthy
rays of the hidden sun, and towards which she will presently
fly in search of adventure if not glorious at least not unworthy.
Her engine warms slowly, emitting a sharp, regular tick like
that of a cheap but sturdy clock. By her side two sleepy
mechanics await my coming. . . . She is gone now, but her
memory brings back a zest of youth. *Ave atque vale.*

XIV

However sorry I might be to abandon the faithful Shorthorn, the new machines soon made me appreciate the
change. For a few days there was no particular craft I
could call my own; I was compelled to make my first flights
on one belonging to Growl. And nervous work it was,
for a bad landing would have brought down upon my head
a torrent of abuse. Several weeks with the Shorthorn had
made it hard to judge distance in a machine with the engine
in front and with the pilot's seat much closer to the ground.
Also the B.E.'s gliding and landing speeds were slightly
greater than those to which I had become accustomed.
What with the difficult aerodrome and my fear of hurting
the machine I had an anxious time, making some very
poor landings at too high a speed.

When, however, I had got the knack of it the machine
became, in comparison to older types, a joy to fly. I had
not altogether forgotten the B.E.s at Gosport, so that I could
relish the increased speed due to the bigger engine as well
as to the improvements in streamline. The engine was
nominally of 90 horse-power, but upon the boss of the four-
bladed propeller was stamped '100 H.P. R.A.F.', which
gave it in my eyes an added importance: it was the highest-
powered engine behind which I had yet flown. And for
her power she ran extraordinarily smoothly and quietly; or
at least it seemed so from the pilot's seat, although I dare
say that the propeller's draught silenced many a startling
rattle which would have been audible had the engine been
behind as in the Shorthorn. Moreover, the exhaust noise was
reduced by two long pipes leading vertically up from the

engine to point like diminutive funnels above the top plane.

In the air the machine was easy to handle, stable, and, once used to her ways, I found her very manœuvrable. She was capable of making vertically banked turns and, I recalled, was strong enough to be looped with safety—inspiring thought! Another, less pleasant thought, was what the pilots at Gosport had said: that she might spin at any moment. But that fatal and mysterious eventuality was, according to Wilhelm and others, unlikely to occur, and as time went on I found out for myself that it was not really to be feared.

The practice flights over, I was sent off again on patrol. Soon I should be wanted for more important work, reconnaissances far over the lines, photography, perhaps even bombing raids, all of which might be productive of much adventure. The one thing I really dreaded was spotting for the artillery; since coming to France I had forgotten the Morse code.

XV

Almost at once Adventure came my way. It seemed indeed that she had been lurking in the clouds, waiting only for me to appear in something more suitable than a Shorthorn. Upon a dawn patrol, I had my first taste of combat with enemy aeroplanes.

It happened towards the end of the morning's work. I had been visiting the northernmost points of the beat when, turning south for the last lap, I noticed some ten miles away a cluster of Archie bursts. With insufficient experience it was hard for me to distinguish our own shell smoke from the enemy's, but it did seem that the firing came from much farther to the west than was usual. It was certainly worth investigating.

Flying south I aimed for a point just ahead of the most recent bursts, rejoicing in the speed of my B.E.2c. At full throttle flying level she made seventy miles an hour; with the nose down but losing only a very little height she would do nearly eighty, whilst in a steady dive she could be counted on for something not far from eighty-five. A fine and fast machine! The only fault to find being that the German machines were considerably faster.

As we sped southwards I pointed out the shell bursts to the observer, indicating the black speck of an aeroplane and making signs that he should get the machine-gun ready for action. The aeroplane I had sighted was turning to the east; I turned still farther to head it off from the lines if it should prove to be an enemy. Ten minutes at full speed brought us close enough to make out the type and national markings. It was British: a B.E. Disappointed I made a turn to the west, slowing down with the intention of cruising around for a little longer before going home.

Below us Archie shells were bursting. I could not make out why. We were some distance from the lines; it could not be at us the guns were firing, nor as far as I could make out at the other B.E. I stared over the side of the fuselage, puzzled.

And then suddenly I saw them. Two German aeroplanes, beneath us, astern and a little to the east. They were almost stationary in relation to us, travelling in the same direction. They looked like venomous insects, the black crosses like the markings on a moth's wing, five hundred feet below. But in front of me the observer still sat facing forward. He had seen nothing. Forgetting that he could not possibly hear, I shouted at the top of my voice: 'Hey! There they are! Fire that bloody gun!' He still faced forward. I banged the top of the fuselage between our two seats, slapped it hard with my open hand. No good. Then I waggled the control stick backwards and forwards to make him move; but I jerked it too fast, the machine did not respond, and I saw those two German machines coming up closer and closer behind us. A nightmare!

At length the observer turned. He was a big man and the violence of his move shook the whole machine; yet he did not turn because he had heard me, but because he heard, as I did too, an ominous *crack-crack* of passing machine-gun bullets.* The machines below were firing at us. I looked down fascinated. The nearest German was about to pass

* It was many years before I appreciated that, with a muzzle-velocity of something over Mach 2, the sound made by passing bullets was a miniature sonic boom.

beneath. Over his top plane I could see an observer in the back seat aiming a machine-gun. I could see the flashes.

The immediate and most urgent problem was to get our own gun in action, for it was in the wrong place, on the forward mounting for use in pursuit. Now that we were the ones pursued it had to be changed to the rear. My signals to the observer were needless, he was already struggling manfully with the unwieldy gun, hampered by the propeller's slipstream, whilst I held to my westerly course, passing right over the first German and only turning a little to let my observer fire a short burst as soon as his gun was ready. Then for a moment the German disappeared under our stern. What was to be done next? I supposed that if the enemy came on after us my observer could deal with him with the gun in the same position. But if I were to circle round and try to attack him the gun would have to be changed again, a tiresome business. Which was it to be?

I hesitated. Not for long, not for more than ten seconds at the outside. And yet when, having decided to hold my course, I looked out over the far side of the fuselage expecting to see the enemy bobbing up alongside I was amazed to find that he had turned back towards the lines. Already he was quite a long way off, and he had stopped firing.

The feeling of mild panic of a few moments previously gave way to an absurd desire for a fight at all costs. Seeing the enemy so close, his murderous-looking gun pointed, shots passing by our heads, I had expected serious trouble. Yet after a score of contemptuous rounds to scare us away he had calmly made off, heading home for his own part of the world. He had done his morning's work, reconnaissance or photography, and now he was going back to tell his friends that he had met a British machine which had turned tail after the first few shots. . . . I had done the wrong thing evidently. I had made a fool of myself by having the gun placed on the rear mounting, by not having turned to attack on first sighting the enemy. My mistake must be remedied and at once. Banking vertically, throttle wide open we started in pursuit.

South of us the second enemy craft was being engaged and chased by the other B.E.; ahead, to the east, our own particular foe was hurrying off in the direction of Lille. I put the nose down, using up the little advantage in height that still remained to us in an attempt to overhaul the enemy. For a few moments he seemed to be rising and moving slowly backwards, the range was decreasing; and while the observer pulled and pushed the Lewis gun into the forward mounting I heard again the *crack-crack* of enemy bullets. . . . At last we were close enough, the Lewis was ready; I started ahead, elated with a wild hope of victory.

But another great difficulty became at once apparent. In a B.E. it was impossible to fire straight forward because of the propeller. The forward gun-mounting gave an arc on either bow, above and below, but to fire straight ahead would be to send shots into the propeller, possibly smashing a blade and consequently bringing the machine down. To hit our enemy we had to turn slightly away from him, put in a burst or two and turn back quickly so as not to open the range.

Accordingly I signalled the observer, and turned off course while he hastily fired off half a drum of ammunition. Then we turned back, nose down to try to close the enemy. But we had no longer any superiority of height from which to dive and gain speed, and on the level the German had an advantage over us of at least ten miles an hour. The range which had been increased by my enforced half turn for firing did not grow less when I turned back in pursuit. On the contrary it began to open up rapidly as the German made for home. The distance between us had never been really short, soon from two hundred yards it lengthened to three hundred, three-fifty, four hundred. The enemy gun ceased fire. We were out of effective range.

Beneath us the open countryside of occupied territory showed that we had come far over the lines. The time for the patrol to end was long past. From fifteen miles away I fancied that I could smell eggs and bacon. And with that I turned the B.E. sharply, setting course for the barge and breakfast.

XVI

Trivial though this fight had been, I discovered shortly after landing that some mystery was connected with it. An uneasy feeling that I had done something wrong came to me; although, thinking the matter over, I believed that I had done everything possible considering my inexperience, yet I was not at all satisfied with the result. Neither, it seemed, was Growl. He said nothing definite, not even as much as on the morning of the balloon attack. But he knew all about the fight before I had a chance to give him my version.

'Where did you first see them?' he asked, meeting me on the way to the barge. 'Did they fire at you? Which way did you turn? Did you see the other two B.E.s?'

I gave him the details as I remembered them—the whole affair was still rather confused in my mind—adding that I had only seen one B.E.

'Only one? You're sure of that?' he insisted.

'As sure as I can be under the circumstances.'

'What circumstances?'

'Well, meeting enemy aircraft for the first time, the excitement of being fired at and of not knowing quite which way to turn or how to get the gun to bear.'

Growl nodded and turned away.

'All right, young fellow. You'll learn in time.'

His tone showed that he was not displeased with what I had done, but he did not choose to enlighten me any further either as to air-fighting or as to the reasons for the questions he had asked. Nor, apparently, was it a subject to be discussed in the mess. I was greeted with an uncomfortable silence when I attempted to raise the matter at breakfast.

Wilhelm told me all about it later. He had not been off the ground that morning and so had been able to listen to the gossip. The trouble about the fight was that there had been two of the squadron's B.E.s close to the enemy when they had first crossed to our side of the lines, long before I had appeared on the scene. One of them, the B.E. I had seen, had attacked immediately, although there had been no need for him to do so since he was on artillery duty. Sticking closely to his enemy he had chased him back over the lines and forced him down. But the rumour was this, that the other B.E. on patrol at the time had taken no notice of the fight, had kept well out of range and had eventually turned right away to steer a straight course back to the squadron. The major was furious, for it was alleged that the pilot of the B.E. which had 'run away' was one of the flight-commanders.

As Hilaire Belloc once sang: 'Due east the foe, due west he steered. . . .'

XVII

It was at about this time that Wilhelm and I, aided by another pilot, started discussing and devising new gun-mountings for our machines.

The B.E., good in her day for so many purposes, was really rather hopeless when it came to aerial combat. The observer, sitting in the front seat, was enclosed by a cage of struts and wires which made it extremely hard not only to handle the gun but also to obtain a clear field of fire. Different mountings for various angles of fire were suggested by the pilots of several squadrons, including our own, and in the majority of machines four of these mountings were adopted as standard. To the underside of the Lewis gun was fitted a blunt spike that could be slipped into a number of different sockets attached to the sides of the observer's cockpit. One of these sockets, like a candle-stick, was fixed just behind the engine, allowing the observer to fire over the top of the propeller; two more, one on either side of the fuselage, gave a small arc on each bow; and, at the back of the front seat, another at the end of a swinging arm afforded protection from the stern. This last mounting was without doubt the best. The observer knelt on his seat with his back to the wind and obtained a good view, the swinging arm gave him a wide arc without him having to move. But it was purely a defensive mounting; its use pre-supposed that the enemy was in pursuit which, except on artillery spotting or during the return from a long recon-naissance, was not a very usual occurrence.

If we intended to attack, pursue and bring down enemy

craft we would have to use the forward gun positions, and
these were inevitably restricted by wires, struts and, most
of all, by the propeller. Only a fortunate chance could give
us the victory we so desired, yet short of reconstructing the
entire machine there was nothing we could do.

As far as protection was concerned it would plainly have
been better to have put the observer in the back seat, as
the Germans had already done, with a revolving mounting;
but as regards attack the only thing for which we could
hope was that someone in England would speedily invent
a means of firing through the propeller. Both the French
and the Germans were reported to be developing different
methods; others were slowly bringing out inventions of their
own; meanwhile the Flying Corps had nothing. Nothing except ideas for new mountings, guns on the wings, guns on
the top plane, new schemes of attack, new aeroplanes—
everything save the solution of the real problem to which,
it seemed, our scientists refused to apply themselves. With
characteristic British skill at compromise, our designers went
so far as to produce an extraordinary craft which in their
fertile brains did away with the problem altogether. It was
called the B.E.9, but the reason for its unofficial name—'The
Pulpit'—was all too obvious. A little three-ply box pro-
jected from the front of the machine, a box supported upon
ball-bearings running on an extension of the propeller shaft
and prevented from rotating by cables to the wingtips.
The wretched man in this box had indeed an unrestricted
forward view, but just behind his head revolved the four
deadly blades of the propeller. There was no communication
possible between front and back seat; if anything happened,
if the pilot were wounded, or even if nothing more serious
occurred than a bad landing in which the machine tipped
over on its nose, the man in the box could but say his
prayers: he would inevitably be crushed by the engine behind
him.

One of these machines was attached to the squadron in
which I served; but by the merciful dispensation of provi-
dence it never succeeded in defeating an enemy craft. Had
it done so I have no doubt that the brains of the Farnborough
factory would have rejoiced in their war-winning discovery,
hundreds of Pulpits would have been produced and in

a short while we should not have had a living observer in France to tell the experts what it was like in that little box. However, even in 1915 when almost every new machine was looked at with delighted wonder, it was recognised that in the B.E.9 unsuitability of design had reached its acme. The Pulpit was soon returned to the depot.

To the faults of the B.E.2c we resolutely shut our eyes, determined with the blind and absurd optimism of youth to make the best of the only aeroplane at our disposal. The more we studied our gun-mountings the more unreasonably hopeful we felt. At nights, after a drink or two in the mess, we grew positively certain of our chances in any fight that might come our way. The omens of the year were favourable: 1415–1915. The fifth centenary of Agincourt! The feast of Crispian was not so far away, and Crispin-Crispian should ne'er go by from this day unto the ending of the world but B.E.s and Lewis guns in it should be remembered. ... Waiter, another beer!

XVIII

By a fortunate succession of accidents my own rôle in the squadron became gradually more that of a fighting pilot than of an artillery spotter or photographer. The first accident occurred when much to my annoyance I was sent off one foggy afternoon to observe for a battery down near La Bassée. Wireless had been fitted to my machine and I had spent a sleepless night trying to remember the Morse code. As soon as we had left the ground I let down the aerial and started nervously to send out my call sign. I went on sending it out at intervals for half an hour whilst cruising around the battery position, wondering why they did not start shooting, until at length I noticed a white strip on the ground informing me that they were not getting my signals. Thinking that probably my poor sending of Morse was responsible for the failure I returned to the squadron in fear and trembling. But there I learnt, much to my relief, that it was the battery's wireless set which had broken down.

The following day was fine, artillery activity was vio-

lently renewed, experienced observers were required. I was
not wanted. Instead I was sent off with a special observer
in Growl's highly polished aeroplane to take a few very
dull photographs of the area behind the Bois de Biez. Photography was uninteresting from my point of view because
there was so little to do; one had to fly slowly over a straight
and clearly defined course taking no notice of Archie or
of enemy aircraft. Of course if one was attacked one defended
oneself, but one did not go off in pursuit—which was what I
most wanted to do.

As a matter of fact there was not a German in the sky
when I went out to take photographs, and Archie was
much more distant than usual. Only one gun seemed to be
in operation; every time we reached the end of our beat he
fired three shells. We took little notice of them.

When we returned to the squadron it was discovered
that all the photographic plates had been put in the wrong
way round. Not a single picture was any good. Had they
all come out it might have been argued that such a steady
and reliable pilot should always be employed upon this
particular job. My career might have been altered, I might
have become a professional photographer. As it was, the
machine was Growl's, the observer (who was to blame)
was Growl's. The job had to be done again, Growl did it.
And the next time I went into the air it was to go upon
a reconnaissance from Lens to Lille.

XIX

I remember that reconnaissance because it was so uneventful that I had all the time necessary to examine the
world spread out beneath me and gain a lasting if super-
ficial impression of the war as it then was in the west.

We were archied when we crossed the lines near Lens,
but after that there were no interruptions as we headed
north over the enemy's back areas. There were no aircraft,
hostile or friendly, to be seen. The sun shone, and the
country below was so peaceful that a momentary fear of my
own wakefulness shook me. I must be asleep, dreaming. The
war was an illusion of my own. Surely the immense and placid

world upon which I gazed could not be troubled by human
storms such as I had been imagining. In that quiet land a
million human beings could never have become so furiously
enraged that they must fly at each other's throats. . . . At
ten thousand feet on a sunny afternoon, with only the keen
wind upon one's face and the hum of an aero-engine in one's
ears, it is hard not to feel godlike and judicial.

We passed over Lille. The great town, marked out by
the angular lines of its old fortifications which had not saved
it from easy capture, looked oddly deserted, dead. What
were they doing down there, those unfortunate French?
Of what were they thinking? What an intolerable nuisance
the war must be for them; not even the more hideous nuisance of active warfare with its compensating hopes and
fears and adventures, just plain unalleviated ennui whilst
their masters walked about proudly, strong in their con-
quest, dealing with them as they willed. From that great
French city there came up a dozen noisy shells to show us
whose it was. Upon the Ronchin aerodrome stood three
aircraft, small as miniature models from our elevation, but
they did not come up. The German held his prize firmly;
there was no need for him to be unnecessarily aggressive.
Circling slowly we turned to the west, leaving the sad town
to bask inactive in the melancholy autumn sunlight.

Over the Messines Ridge we flew, to recross the lines near
Wytshaete; but before turning homewards it struck me that
here was a good opportunity to learn the line as far as
the coast. We headed north following the curve of the
Ypres salient, and at once Archie reopened, accompanying
us on either side. Far below, at some two or three thousand
feet from the ground, another avenue of Archie puffs was
growing. I found the machine at which he was firing, just
distinguishable as a B.E. twisting and dodging to avoid
the shells. At our level the fire became heavier as we approached the neighbourhood of Ypres, but on the ground,
save for a rare flash, a puff of dust or smoke, nothing seemed
to be happening. Our own artillery, of course, was always
said to be short of anmmunition, yet now the Germans
were not firing either. Were *they* running short of ammunition
or were they merely bored? Nothing to fire at on the ground so
they amused themselves by wasting their precious shells in the

air. I tried to count those that had been fired since we left Lille. It was impossible. There were too many. The sky behind us was mottled with fading puffs. A score, two, three score? One might be nearer the truth if one estimated more than a hundred. And not half a dozen had come within the range where a chance splinter would have strength enough to do serious damage. Once or twice I had turned to one side or the other, had changed altitude a little to make sure that the gunners should have no time to improve their aim; but never, during this flight at least, had the bursting shells given me cause for alarm; from the objectives of the reconnaissance they had not forced us to deviate by so much as a hair's breadth. In the air a futile bombardment; in the trenches nothing more than occasional gun-fire.

In front of Ypres the sector was a little more active than other parts of the line, but still strangely silent. The opposing armies faced each other motionless in the disarray of their diggings as though puzzled, now that they had levelled everything within sight, as to how they could work further mischief. Again I was struck by the immensity, the colossal size not merely of the war (of which one could judge at home by adding up the totals of the armed men engaged), but of these ruinous digging operations. I stared back along the route we had been following. For league upon league and from either side the zig-zag trails rushed forward, branching, rejoining, intersecting one another like forked lightning. The turned soil was pale upon the brown surface of the earth, so that the vast disturbance showed up plainly, even in the haze of distance, like the breaking waves of a frozen sea, the two fronts facing each other like rival oceans beating vainly upon an interminable isthmus. That narrow strip of land between the foaming waves of trenches resisted staunchly, its shores bound with wire, its surface only a little marked by the splashes of shell-fire. No Man's Land—the name took on a new significance. For only where no man could live was the earth permitted, in a measure, to survive.

To the north were flooded fields, covered with shallow water, dark brown, stagnant . . . Stagnant? The whole line was that, the whole western front, the whole war! The hard-pressed line around tragic Ypres told a simple story. We held it because we had made a stand there, because it was the last town in Belgium, because of the moral effect. Yes, but from my aeroplane seat I saw the Channel ports. So close! There lay the sea. But I saw no ships. The long lines of ripples advancing slowly to break in foam upon the sandy coast were as deserted as the lines of trenches, almost as motionless. Would we ever attack that bleak coast? I wondered. Or had we had enough of such landings after the experience of the Dardanelles? Even there it seemed the war had come to a standstill.

XX

I encountered the major that evening after I had landed. There was no avoiding him.

'I saw you do a spiral glide,' he said in a melancholy voice. 'You were making quite a steep bank too. You must remember that towards forty-five degrees the rudder tends to become the elevator and helps you to keep the nose up. Your glide was quite nice to watch. But you really must take more care over your landings.'

At the first words of unexpected appreciation a novel feeling of friendliness had come to me, but his final remark took away all pleasure. I had made an abominable landing. He went on to tell me what I should do in order to make a good one. As if I didn't know! If he had laughed or rated me soundly for a clumsy pilot, a second-rate artist, I should have understood it. It was the toneless pedantry of voice and the reserve of manner that awoke my faint resentment. He made no comment on the flight from which I had just returned, but proffered with a frozen tongue some general observations on not landing too fast, on not landing too slow, on gliding in straight and on judging the distance accurately. And then he turned away, walking off with long, rather high-stepping strides, turning his head inquisitively from side to side, more like a lonely bird than ever.

I sat on the ground to remove my leather flying-kit. The officer with the distressing complaint passed by.

'What was that old Starched Shirt talking to you about?' he wanted to know.

'Oh, nothing much. Just complaining about my bad landing.'

'Well, I like his impudence! The last time he made a landing he almost broke his neck!'

He went on to state that in his opinion the Starched Shirt was a blot on our horizon. And not only in his opinion, but in that of the squadron as well. Smarting under criticism of my flying, I thought—with youthful bumptiousness and pride —that the squadron was probably not far wrong.

XXI

In the barge Wilhelm grabbed my arm and drew me into his cabin.

'I've done it!' he exclaimed in an excited whisper.

'Done what?' I asked, catching some of his excitement.

'Looped! This afternoon—well away from the lines, behind Armentières.'

'Good work—what was it like?'

'Frightful! I was scared stiff. But it wasn't really so difficult. I've forgotten exactly what I did, but I'll tell you about it later when I've had time to think it out. For Heaven's sake don't tell anyone else!'

'Of course not,' I replied emphatically. 'If Growl got to know he'd throw a fit. And the major would probably send you home under arrest.'

From looping we went on to talk and argue about the intricacies of flying as we knew them. Apart from the mysteries of spinning there was still much that was unexplored, and we young pilots could still improve our art by discussing all that we had seen and heard, by evolving our own theories, and by practising in the air manœuvres that were neither taught nor encouraged. What of looping? Would it help us fight? Would it tend to improve our ability in the air?

The Germans had brought out a new fighting craft: a Fokker monoplane with a rotary engine. It was fast, very manœuvrable, with a gun firing through the propeller by means of a mechanism captured, it was said, from the French. For these good reasons the machine was proving almost certain death to our B.E.s, particularly when it was flown by a German pilot named Immelmann. Very vaguely it was being rumoured that this young officer (who had already brought down the incredible number of six machines) had invented a new method of turning. As a matter of fact I believe he never did any such thing, but he certainly had a remarkably clever way of throwing his machine around so as to appear suddenly, almost sitting on his enemy's tail, with his machine-gun banging away straight through the propeller. The 'Immelmann Turn' it was beginning to be called, and it opened up a new set of problems in aerial fighting.

It was not so long since machines of the Longhorn type had sidled gingerly past one another firing with rifles at a safe range of half a mile or more. Some of us still carried rifles for there was a shortage of guns, but the principle of machine-guns for all aircraft had long been recognised. A few machines were occasionally allowed to carry two guns, although one would have been just as good had we been able to fire through the propeller. The Fokker announced the first phase of a new era. Through-propeller firing was an accomplished fact, and, coupled with the type of aeroplane in which it was being used, was forcing upon us new ideas, new tactics. To bring down an enemy machine of any type required luck, persistence, a fast aeroplane, and a well-aimed machine-gun; but to bring down the Fokker or even to defend oneself successfully against it required something much more. It required from the scientist a better war machine.

Sometimes we would talk far into the night, waiting hopefully for the fine morning when we might start practising these new ideas that were to guard us against the menace of the Fokker.

XXII

But now again for several days of appalling weather there was no flying. No machines of any sort, let alone enemies to test our prowess, were to be seen in the damp and foggy skies. The days passed in dull wanderings about the aerodrome, in lengthy and fruitless visits to the hangars where our aeroplanes stood silent in the clammy darkness from which it seemed that they would never emerge. Games other than ping-pong were seldom played in that squadron; horses were difficult to obtain. A long walk in the rain followed by a long drink in the mess would often form the sole recreation of an entire day.

After one dreary evening I remember how Wilhelm leaned back with a sigh: 'Oh dear, oh dear—what a bloody life this is, anyway!'

I agreed, but asked him what constituted the particular 'bloodiness' he had in mind.

'Oh—the uselessness and flatness of it all,' he answered, frowning at not being able to express his feelings more eloquently.

I agreed again, remarking that we hadn't been in the air for three days and that it didn't seem to matter to anyone if we stayed on the ground for three days more.

'The trouble is,' I added, 'that no one gives us anything to do.'

'What do you expect?' retorted Wilhelm. 'Since the Loos offensive failed, no one has done anything anywhere. Hundreds of unfortunate men die in trenches every day—uselessly and almost accidentally—but otherwise we might just as well be at peace. And now this damned weather stops even our flying.'

'I wonder,' I put in, 'if anyone in this squadron really cares if we bring down an enemy or not?'

Wilhelm grunted scornfully.

'Foxy and one or two others would sooner we didn't—they have their own reputations to think of.'

I remarked gloomily that for the sake of something to do I would almost prefer to return to the infantry. But the remark was made in exasperation; I did not really mean it, and Wilhelm was quick to protest.

'The infantry are having a rotten time, but they're not doing any more good in the trenches than we are in the air. I tell you fighting, serious fighting, is over until next spring. And the only thing for us to do is to go on looking for trouble until we get shot down or spin into the ground. Foxy is right—we shall probably end by being *carboneezay*. . . .'

Everyone, I suppose, groused in that way at some time

or another. It did not mean very much and it made no
difference to the length of the war.

XXIII

A few dull flights in bad weather, a few patrols productive of nothing more exciting than a little inaccurate
Archie, and then the tedium was unexpectedly broken. In
surprisingly rapid succession several aerial combats came my
way.

They are no longer of any account, those fights whose
importance, small enough at the time, has faded altogether
with the years. Their very similarity makes them monotonous to relate, robs them of the last vestiges of specious
glamour with which we then surrounded them as with a halo
of glory. Today there can be but one reason for describing
such fights in any detail, the mild excuse of historical interest. Aerial fighting as it was in those days will never be
seen again. The machines in which we fought are as antiquated as the three-deckers of Nelson's day, the methods and
conditions of fighting so primitive as to seem unreal, even
ridiculous. Of all that time not much is left other than a
few memories of adventure, zestful enough to stimulate even
now a quicker beat of the pulse.

And it does not add to the story of these occasions to
have to admit that in the course of my next three fights I
failed to bring down a single enemy. Each combat began as
a pursuit above the trenches, was continued beyond the
lines, and ended by the enemy descending to take refuge
upon the territory of his own aerodrome. It could scarcely
be otherwise. At this period of the war the German two-
seaters had orders to leave fighting to the fighting craft
(Fokkers and such) and not to become involved in scraps
which formed no part of their work of reconnaissance or
photography. They were very wise. Their missions accomplished, it was their duty to return safely with the information they had gathered and not to waste time bandying
bullets with marauding British craft. They had in any case
to run the gauntlet of our machines which, save on special
occasions, were expected to engage any hostile aeroplane

sighted. The German tactic of turning away formed a sound policy which often lured our machines to their doom.

One day on patrol I decided to climb my B.E. up to her maximum altitude. In the squadron, M.C. had been much admired a week or so previously for having taken his machine to a height of 12,000 feet, and at the time it had indeed seemed a remarkable performance. Nevertheless, having passed the 10,000 mark in the Shorthorn, I felt confident of getting a good deal higher. For an hour I dragged my aeroplane skywards and, after passing through a layer of scattered clouds, at length emerged in sunshine at a height —according to the untrustworthy aneroid—of 14,000 feet. But here it was so bitterly cold that it was plainly useless to dally unless something in the nature of an enemy turned up pretty swiftly.

Far to the east and considerably below us a diminutive white wing gleamed in the sunlight, turned and became an indistinct speck. An enemy? Mighty far away whatever he was, hardly worth while investigating. I tilted the machine backwards and forwards to attract the observer's attention. He turned to face me; and I got a shock. Both cheeks and the tip of his nose were dead white, frozen. His eyes, too, were rimmed with ice; he kept rubbing them but they seemed to freeze over again immediately, and he had such difficulty in moving that it took no more than a glance to see that he was in a bad way. I throttled down at once and began to glide.

At 14,000 feet over northern France in November one realised how very exposed were the seats of a B.E. I was thoroughly chilled myself and I had a windscreen, whereas the observer's had been removed to make room for the forward gun-mounting. With the engine running slowly it was possible to make oneself heard, I shouted to ask how he felt. He turned, trying to grin; but his face was stiff, he could barely move his jaw enough to shout something back at me. I only got the one word: 'Awful'; sufficient to make me push the stick forward for a faster descent.

One of the disadvantages of flying so high was that it seemed to take such a long time to come down, especially as I had to run the engine every now and then to make sure that it was not getting too cold. Had we met an enemy

during that glide we would have had to run for it; the
observer could never have handled the gun with frozen fingers.
It did not begin to be noticeably warmer until we were
below 6,000 feet, but I went on down and did not flatten
out until we were at three thousand. In contrast with the
height at which we had been the machine now seemed to
be dangerously low, almost on the ground, but the air was
like summer. And a little later when Archie opened fire
the air became warmer still.

The long glide had taken us to the southern sector of the
line; we were over the La Bassée Canal, where in the greenish
water of the dock basin a string of barges were moored—
when straight ahead, near the disturbed area of the Loos
battlefield, an aeroplane materialised as if by magic. Unmistakably an enemy, and an unusual one at that: it was
Two Tails himself.*

Two Tails was very much of a *rara avis*, a machine of
mystery. As far as I know he had not been seen more than
two or three times, had been fought (indecisively) only once.
In general appearance he bore a slight resemblance to a
Shorthorn, much improved and modernised. Instead of
a bare framework of tail-booms he had two neat streamline
fuselages supporting the rudders and tail-plane. He was
reputed to carry at least three machine-guns and, according
to Foxy, 'half a dozen gentlemen in top-hats' (meaning
crash-helmets) by way of crew. At all events he was fast,
with a Mercédès engine giving probably double the power
of the 'R.A.F.', and therefore with a much better climb
than the B.E. On the only occasion when he had been
seriously engaged there had been terrific descriptions in the
British press, and a full-page drawing in an illustrated paper
of this new and fearsome strong-man of the skies. At the
sight of him, glinting in the pale yellow sunlight that il-
luminated the hazy battlefield, banking to dodge a cluster
of British Archie shells, I felt the sort of alarming thrill that
might run through the crew of a merchantman on encoun-
tering an enemy battle-cruiser.

The observer, now completely thawed out, had seen
him too and turned to point, an anxious question in his
eyes. I waved frantically, the gun was transferred to the

* Later identified as the 'Ago CIII.'

forward mounting, and we started off in pursuit like ornitho-
logists after a little-known specimen. At the start our courses
converged so that almost immediately I began to hear a
quick *crack-crack, crack-crack* as of two machine-guns. Then,
as we came within range, our own gun began to clatter
and—the observer's aim must have been good—Two Tails
made a violent swerve, turning almost at right-angles to
head north-east across the lines.

Conforming to his movement I made the mistake of trying to climb up to his height (he was about five hundred
feet higher) and this, together with a turn aside for the observer to fire again, deprived us of any chance we might
have had of bringing him down near the lines. As we climbed
the range opened out, changing in a few minutes, during
which my observer could not put in a single shot, from two
to five hundred yards. After that it increased still more
rapidly, for Two Tails was no longer climbing. On the
contrary, finding himself safely over his own territory he
was pushing his nose down to gain speed and outdistance
us. Our only possibly reply was to do likewise even at the
risk of losing a safe height over enemy country. We had
gained about a thousand feet since the beginning of the
engagement; now we commenced to descend again, pushing
on at full throttle at a speed approaching eighty miles an
hour. To all appearance Two Tails became stationary, then
began to move slowly backwards; the range was shortening.

But the chase lasted a long time and at the swift pace
we were travelling I could see a dark and misty patch of
buildings. We were coming close to Lille. It was essential
to do something quickly for we were being drawn much too
far over the enemy's territory. I pointed, waved to the observer, making signs for him to shoot. He must have been
expecting my suggestion, for he nodded and opened fire
at once—through the propeller.

It was not quite such a foolish thing to do as might be
imagined. What the exact odds were against smashing the
propeller I cannot say; they depended a great deal upon the
engine speed and its relation to the gun's rate of fire. I
seemed to remember having heard that the number of shots
likely to hit one of the blades was in the neighbourhood of
four per cent, and as my observer would not be able to fire

more than about thirty rounds I believed that we could get away with it, particularly since there was no certainty that the propeller would break if hit. Cases had been known of enemy bullets piercing the blades neatly and without splintering the wood.

As it happened I think my observer got off some twenty-five rounds before I felt a faint shock and slightly increased vibration of the engine, indicating that he had hit the propeller. Then, quickly turning off course to prevent any further damage from our own fire, I watched the enemy. Two Tails had also turned, but away from us. Evidently our fire had been accurate and he did not like it. He was going down.

There seemed to be nothing wrong with his manner of descent, save that it was too fast for me to follow; the range was opening out once more and he did not appear to be bothering about us at all, his guns were silent. Looking ahead I soon perceived the reason: the Ronchin aerodrome was less than two miles off, he was gliding home to lunch; if I did not take care we would be his unwilling guests, for our height was under three thousand and Ronchin was full of waiting aircraft. Someone might be sent up to invite us to the meal. The place was the reputed home of the fabled Immelmann.

The very thought of that dangerous young man's nearness made me crane my neck to search the heavens for possible foes, guiltily remembering that I should have looked sooner had I not been so intent on the chase. And then I caught my breath. Three or four thousand feet above us, hovering—so it seemed—hawklike in the sky was a swart monoplane. A Fokker!

My observer was still hanging half out of his seat, his eyes glued upon Two Tails; the sharpness of my turn almost flung him out altogether. Bumping heavily back into the cockpit he gave me a reproachful glance, whilst I jerked my hand upwards over my head. He stared for a moment and I saw the look on his face change from surprise to anxiety. Then without further ado he began to wrestle with the gun, tugging it clear of wires and struts and dumping it upon the rear, defensive mounting. He was a sharp lad and knew what was wanted.

Fortunately for us the Fokker was a long way up and dived neither very fast nor very steeply, whereas with the throttle hard open, nose well down, we were rattling home at a really tremendous speed—over eighty-five—straight for the nearest point of the lines. The observer watched anxiously astern, occasionally loosing off a few rounds as a warning that we were not to be caught napping. Perhaps some of those shots came close enough to annoy him. At all events, a mile or so from the lines he turned away to climb back towards the east, leaving us at only two thousand feet to be escorted over the trenches by a lengthening trail of Archie bursts.

XXIV

'Hm . . .' murmured the major, smiling whimsically as though at a mild but rather subtle joke. 'And so you met Two Tails, did you? What was he like?' So might an awkward child have recited: *And hast thou slain the Jabberwock?* But there was no *Come to my arms* in his tone. He continued, 'I hear you followed him across the lines? Was he much faster than your machine? Why didn't you follow him to Lille?'

The questions were put calmly, but with slightly more than the usual amount of interest. I answered his last by explaining the proximity of a dangerous enemy.

'Saw a Fokker, eh? Ah, then I suppose you did right to come back. But all this must have taken place very low down. You should be careful never to cross the lines at less than six thousand feet.' (Heavens! thought I, having crossed them twice that morning at under three.) 'You had better make out a report of your fight. . . .'

He sauntered off, pleased but absent.

.   .   .   .   .

'Hullo! Had a scrap?' Wilhelm came towards me, grinning cheerfully. 'What—with Two Tails? You're lucky to be alive! How many machine-guns did he have?'

'I don't know,' I told him truthfully. 'I never had a clear

view of him. The propeller was in the way all the time.'

'Then how did you see to fire at him?'

'Ah—you must ask my observer that!'

.   .   .   .   .   .

From behind me heavy footsteps drew near.

'Now then, young fellow,' Growl exclaimed truculently, 'how the devil did you manage to get two bullets through that propeller of yours?'

His voice was menacing, he looked as if he might bite.

'I had a scrap.'

'Damn it, I know you did. But where did those bullets come from? The enemy?'

'Er—yes, I think so.'

'Nonsense! Don't try to tell *me* that story. Those shots came from your own gun! You'll have to get a new propeller, and these things cost money. Don't you know that? How would you like it if the Government said that *you* had to fork out forty pounds?' I kept quiet while he scowled angrily at me for a second or two, then slowly his features relaxed into a tolerant smile. 'Well, all right. Go and make out your report.'

.   .   .   .   .

On the way to the barge I passed M.C. He was whistling and slashing the heads of thistles with a cane made from the propeller of the German aeroplane he had brought down in the summer. Except to answer my 'good morning', he said nothing. I wanted very much to tell him that I had beaten his height record, but I felt too shy to break down his stony reserve. In this squadron taciturnity was the best policy.

XXV

No more than three days later I had the luck to run into another fight in the air. But this time the engagement was very brief and uneventful, and it was Archie who played the major part with almost fatal consequences.

Captivity: beginning—St Quentin gaol, December, 1915. Author extreme left, observer right

Captivity: end—Dutch frontier, 17 April 1918. Beverley
Robinson left, author right

An observer was sent with me who was no novice and needed no practice flights to get the hang of things. In the earlier days of the war his machine had been brought down in Holland; he had only recently escaped from internment, all the keener for his enforced rest. On the early patrol we went straight across the lines in the neighbourhood of the Bois de Biez.

For once there were quite a few machines about and it was hard to know which of the many specks to investigate first. At least it seemed certain that over British territory there was as yet nothing doing, it was too early; no Archie bursts signalled the presence of enemy aircraft. At length, however, above the Aubers Ridge we sighted a grey two-seater of foreign design heading towards our lines, and we were nearing eight thousand feet, with the other a little higher, when I first made out the black crosses on the underside of his wings. Not that I had for a moment believed him to be British, but in the days before national markings were clearly and prominently displayed, Frenchmen in new and unfamiliar types of craft had sometimes been fired at. . . .

As soon as we were sure of his identity I turned away, hoping to inveigle him across our lines before attacking. By that time I should have gained height and if we could outfight him we stood a chance of bringing him down upon our side of the trenches. But we had no luck. I suppose he must have seen us and suspected our motives from the start, for he made a sharp turn, came straight towards us and opened fire, putting his first few shots through the wings. Our gun was on the rear mounting at the time, and, as he circled almost over our heads, the observer gave him a long burst. This seemed to decide him for he straightened out of the turn and made for home. On the same level we exchanged shots, then he dived away to the east. My observer switched the gun to the forward mounting and once again a pursuit commenced.

On this as on other occasions the chase led to Ronchin. It seemed indeed as though the enemy had planned to lure any and every attacking aeroplane to Lille and I watched the sky anxiously, blinking at the rising sun, thinking it likely that a Fokker might be waiting for us. The eastern heavens appeared to be empty, but Archie was wide awake,

D

warning anyone who happened to be about and giving us
a foretaste of what we must expect on the return journey.
On the way out we scarcely fired a shot. The range was
excessive and, with Growl's admonition in mind we could
not risk firing through the propeller. Only once did I hear
bullets coming close to us, but they did no damage; our
pursuit continued at greater speed as the German airman
increased the angle of his descent.

At length it became apparent that, short of landing at
Ronchin and fighting it out with our fists, we should never
catch up. As I flattened out and started to turn, the observer
put in one more burst of fire to make sure that the enemy
did not return to bother us, and then transferred the gun
to the rear mounting. A last glance when we had settled on
the homeward course showed us the German throttling
down and making as if to land. The fight was over, Lille
was alongside, now we had Archie to contend with.

He was certainly lively and uncommonly accurate that
morning. So much so that after only a few rounds had been
fired I realised that we should have to start dodging in
earnest. Chasing to the east had reduced our altitude considerably, in fact we were now at the right height for Archie
to do his dirtiest work, but I could not for the life of me
remember what procedure was recommended as the best
means of fooling the gunners. How often did one turn? How
long did one wait after turning? Did one alter one's height
just after a shell had burst or just before? 'After', might be
too late; but how did one know when it was just 'before'?

A succession of shells banged out on either hand. Cast
iron splinters flew from yellow smoke balls. Small clicking
vibrations in the body of the machine told that she was being
hit. Two more bursts. I looked forward. There was a dent
in the engine cowling, a tear in the fabric of one wing.
Nothing serious as yet, but we had to get away from this.
Abruptly I turned, at right-angles, away from the lines; held
the new course for half a minute, turned back at right-angles;
throttled down to dive several hundred feet off our altitude.
The next salvo of shells exploded at a more generous distance.
I was reassured, but we were not safe yet and I kept the
engine at half throttle to lose still more height.

And then, above the roaring of the wind, I heard a strange

hooting noise, rising to an alarming shriek. I stared forward uneasily. What the deuce was happening? Had the observer been wounded? He was leaning back, his knees drawn up to allow his feet to rest upon the forward gun-mounting; with one of his hands he waved his flying-cap over his head. He was singing—no, I beg his pardon; he was a cavalry officer and he was making huntin' noises. At every Archie shot he waved his cap again and gave a terrific view-halloo! I don't know how he had the nerve. Personally I was feeling cold and ill. . . .

Archie got the new range. A shell burst sickeningly close, sending a big jagged fragment to smash against an inter-plane strut. A foot-long wooden splinter chipped off, the strut vibrated like a rope drawn suddenly taut. If it gave we were finished. . . . In front of me I caught sight of a grinning face. 'Yoicks!' yelled the observer.

XXVI

Going aboard the barge I ran into Foxy. I was carrying the damaged strut from my machine, intending to hang it up in my cabin as a reminder of what Archie might sometimes do. He eyed it grimly, then smiled and chuckled with a little shake of the head that implied a hopeless view of my case.

'Fire-eating again? Oh, you make me go all "goosey"— you're too hot for me, altogether too hot. You won't last long at this rate, you'll soon "go west", see if you don't— *tee-hee!*'

His manner of speaking, shivering with mock terror, was really very comical, and he was a very senior flight-com-mander so of course I laughed heartily. But I hid my strut and waited until the mess was nearly empty before going in.

I found Wilhelm alone at the breakfast table.

'You lucky beggar!' he muttered. 'Another fight? You'll be getting ahead of me, if I'm not careful. What does the major think of it?'

'How do you expect *me* to know?' I answered. 'He doesn't say anything much. He seemed particularly listless this morning.'

'Listless? Ah, that's because of the King.'

'Why? What about the King?'

'Well, he's in France, inspecting and visiting troops and trenches.'

'Yes, I know—but he doesn't want to see the major, does he?'

Wilhelm grinned and shook his head.

'I'm sure he doesn't. But the point is that H.M. is due somewhere in this vicinity tomorrow afternoon and we have to be in the air patrolling. You and I go up after lunch.'

XXVII

With romantic thoughts of the fierce combats we might have to endure in the course of protecting the King, we worked ourselves into a state of considerable excitement, and had some luckless enemy wandered across the lines that day the quality of our mercy would not have been strained, for we would have shown him none. But it was the weather that kept the peace in the air. From early morning it grew steadily worse. Heavy layers of grey cloud sank momentarily lower as they drifted by like partially deflated balloons, just high enough to clear the upper branches of the poplars, whilst over the farm and down the Lys there rolled slowly from the north a yellowish mist. English fog had escorted His Majesty across the Channel. At noon thin rain commenced to fall.

Upon all normal occasions such weather would have been labelled totally unfit for flying, but on this day not only were we expected to fly, we were keen to do so. I confess without shame that, as my machine rushed down that curving strip of an aerodrome towards a barely visible row of trees I felt a pang of very real anxiety. What would happen when I was off the ground if already I could not so much as see the treetops? And what should I do when the mists closed in about me, obscuring all view of the earth? Blind flying was not a thing any young pilot cared to undertake in those days; there was too great a likelihood of a turn developing into a spin. And I could not imagine how I was to find my way back to the squadron, or indeed to any other safe landing-ground.

But no sooner were we away, clear of all immediate obstructions, than I began to regain confidence. True, at five hundred feet we encountered the first cloudbank, but it was quite thin and through many large gaps I could see the darkened earth streaked with familiar fields and streams. Circling the aerodrome, we climbed rapidly to the second layer. It was not more than a few hundred feet above the first, yet the black clouds were thick and closely knit together, so that I had much difficulty in finding a space through which to fly.

My orders were to patrol at a height of roughly eight to ten thousand feet, but as it appeared unlikely that we should ever get so high I should have been justified in returning after a short flight to report that the weather was hopeless. Yet now, at a comparatively safe altitude, I was lured on to explore the mystery of those lowering clouds. No more perhaps than a wish for adventure, a need to get away from the tedium of the small world below; but there was also in me a desire to seek a fight on this of all days. Of course the fact that M.C. was already flying somewhere in the mists spurred me on, too; I had no intention of being outflown by him. But there was no time to waste in puzzling out the reasons for wanting to go on, steering the B.E. through the unfrequent cloud gaps held all my attention.

Dodging the larger masses, driving through the smaller ones when it was inevitable, we climbed steadily and at length reached a vast grey space between two main layers of seemingly impenetrable vapour. Shut off from the sky as well as from the earth it seemed now as if the world had passed forever from our ken, as if, over some endless desolate plain of Inferno, I, the Virgil-guide, were conducting to a scene of eternal sorrow my observer Dante. A glimpse of his profile reassured me: stolid, unimaginative, beefy, unmistakably British. Yet the illusion persisted. I climbed higher to seek others.

Only once during the ascent did we get any prolonged sight of the ground. From five thousand feet I peered through a gap in the several layers, and with the help of the map made out that we were over a clearing in the Forêt de Nieppe, the very point from which the patrol was to radiate. Ten minutes to the north and south of this clearing, with a few minutes extra one way to allow for the wind, that was to be the limit of our flying for two hours. I began hurriedly comparing watch, air-speed and compass, setting the throttle to obtain an exact number of revolutions while climbing. The gap passed astern, the damp mists closed in about us. Heavy rain drove by, soaking Dante.

There were no more gaps either up or down and it soon became apparent that we were involved in the main bank. I was uneasy, for this mass of clouds might well extend to fifteen or twenty thousand feet, far above the utmost ceiling of the B.E. Should I continue to climb with the unpleasant prospect of having to return through the same mass, or should I throttle down and terminate the patrol at once? Whilst I yet hesitated, time went by. The first ten-minute period was almost up, I had to make a turn. Easier said than done. It was quite possible to steer a fairly straight course for a while by watching the instruments and by keeping the control stick steady in the position which I knew would give the best climb. But in these dense clouds the slightest bump tended to alter the course unnoticeably by putting on a small amount of bank, starting a turn. And then it became difficult to judge the amount of pressure required on the rudder-bar; the turn might increase, or it might develop in the other direction. A sudden raising of the speed might denote that the nose was down; it might also be caused by a sharp downward turn. To pull the stick back then might bring on a spin.

Fortunately at exactly the end of ten minutes the clouds thinned out before us, we flew on into a large irregularly shaped cavity. Jagged grey walls, massive in their imposing thickness, surrounded us; a little sickly yellow light came from the roof, but the gloom was awe-inspiring. We were at nearly eight thousand feet and there was no sign of the end, of the beginning of blue sky. Carefully, I turned the machine round and drove back into the wall of vapour.

A violent bump lifted my right wing. I corrected it slowly. A wave of air rolled beneath the other wing and I felt a forward tilt as though the tail were lifting. The air-speed went up. Very gently I eased back the stick, steadying the machine until I judged that she was once more on an even keel and a straight course. Minutes passed whilst I strained my eyes through the fog. And all at once I perceived a dim white shape just above us: faintly luminous, circling swiftly, hovering as though about to dive. Another machine? An enemy? Or some unknown horror of the air, something that could see through the clouds, that had the advantage of us in speed?

Giddiness and tremendous relief came to me at one and the same time. The sun! We were coming through the clouds; and we were turning. Turning—the circle was so narrow that had I pulled the stick back another inch we must at once have gone into a spin. We were turning at speed, yet before sighting that livid disc neither I nor my observer had noticed anything wrong. . . . Cloud-flying, before the days of turn-indicators, was a mystifying business.

Hastily I straightened up, grinning at Dante, and a minute or two later we came out into bright sunlight at a height of nine thousand feet. All about and above us lay huge tumbled mountains of cumulus, not snow-white today, for at an immensely greater height a final layer of misty cirrus was stretched like a golden veil across the sun, but rose-tinted where the light struck them, orange-brown in the shadow, dark blue in the clefts and hollows. Upon the greatest of the towering clouds our own shadow was cast, encircled by a wide halo of rainbow hues. The summit of that nebulous mountain was rounded, sculptured with perfect symmetry—vast as Coleridge's 'stately pleasure dome'. The analogy was easy to follow. . . . At its foot nestled the white houses of Xanadu. Southward, across a level brown plain, drifted the dust of Kublai Khan's horsemen. And beside me, in a black and terrifying canyon with walls five thousand feet deep ran Alph, the Sacred River, flowing through caverns not altogether measureless to man, since I could unromantically check their depths with the aneroid, but undeniably down to a sunless world wherein deluded humans fought in darkness for ideals as brightly coloured as these very clouds. . . . In the front seat Dante shifted awkwardly and dried the Lewis gun with a pocket handkerchief.

Climbing gradually to eleven thousand feet we patrolled up and down for the better part of an hour. Not a single aeroplane, hostile or friendly, was to be seen, and, considering the state of the weather at lower levels, I became convinced that by now all good German pilots must be comfortably at rest in their quarters exchanging *Prosits* and playing *skat*. No use waiting for them. I must go home. Diving through Alph's impressive gorge, I left the bright world of one poet's dreams to return to the dim Inferno of another's. It rained all the way down; Dante was drenched to the skin.

When at one thousand feet I obtained a clear sight of the ground what I saw was not reassuring. We were over woods, but I could not recognise them, neither could Dante. Beneath the clouds and in pouring rain we came lower, to within two hundred feet of the earth. I saw a farmhouse, a small stream, a ploughed field bordered by trees; all were unfamiliar. A horrible doubt crossed my mind—that we might have been blown across the lines whilst flying in that world of illusion above the mists. Could this be German territory? For nearly two hours we had been out of sight of the earth; although I had tried to allow for a possible west wind, it would require very little error to take us ten fatal miles to the east. With growing anxiety I scanned the few landmarks, still without recognising any of them. Visibility was bad. Before risking a further increase in our possible error we must be bold enough to land and ask the way. French peasants would help us wherever we might be. Turning into wind, I came down in the ploughed field and taxied up to the farmhouse.

In spite of the rain, one or two bedraggled people came from the building, plodding slowly towards us through the mud. I beckoned furiously to hasten their lagging feet, shouting to know where we were. They looked at us with gaping mouths as if we were monsters from another planet. They did not seem to know of any of the places for which we asked. At length I mentioned Merville; and at that a young farmer smiled broadly and pointed through the driving rain. In the direction of his outstretched hand I made out a church spire and the black hump of many houses, half-obscured by fog. It was my turn to gape. Merville—not a quarter of a mile away! We were under two miles from the aerodrome.

We waved our thanks, taxied stickily through the muddy field and took off. . . .

The other patrol flights, including M.C., had landed long before us. We had tea alone and in comfort. My observer, ex-Dante, sighed as he relaxed into an armchair.

'I made sure you were going to land us in Germany,' he said cheerfully.

In the evening we heard the news. The King had been seriously hurt by his horse rearing and falling upon him.

XXVIII

In the barge one day, I found Wilhelm examining a large-scale map of north-eastern France. At his side was another pilot from the same flight, a serious lad whose hobby it was to collect what he termed 'rare earths'. I am ignorant enough not to know what sort of 'ologist this made him, but he claimed that it was a very exciting study. Once, when he made a forced landing upon a heap of manure, it was generally supposed that not engine trouble but the needs of his peculiar vocation had brought him down. He was a very good pilot, but inclined to lord it over me because he had one hundred and fifty hours' flying to his credit, whereas at that time I had no more than seventy.

'What would you do,' he asked as I came in, 'if you had to come down on the far side of Valenciennes?'

I replied, I think, that I had not yet considered the problem, no one having invited me to go so far.

'There's nothing to laugh at,' I was told. 'You ought to start thinking about it right away. This squadron does the Long Reconnaissance next week and it's the turn of our flight to go.'

'But I thought it was Foxy's turn?'

'No, his Flight did it last time. And besides, Foxy is leaving the squadron. He has had some sort of row with the major. So *we* do the Long Reco.—and *you'll* probably have plenty of chances to indulge in your favourite pastime of air-fighting!'

I asked to be enlightened for this particular reconnaissance was known to me by name only. I wanted details, and I knew that Rare Earths would take a spiteful pleasure in announcing them. He was going on leave in a few days' time.

'You fly south from here,' he explained, 'cross the lines between Lens and Arras at the greatest height your machine can get to, pass over Douai, Orchies, Denain, Anzin and Valenciennes, circling each place—slowly, mind you—so that your observer can take notes and count the rolling-stock in the railway stations. Then you turn round and come back, well to the south so as to avoid Douai like the plague, recross the lines if you're lucky and come home.'

'Sounds rather tiresome,' said Wilhelm. 'But what's the matter with Douai?'

Rare Earths chuckled.

'Well, it so happens that the Germans have put a full-size aerodrome there. When they see you go over on the way out, they stand by to wait for you on the return. And it's not very nice to find half a dozen Fokkers sitting on your tail when you're heading back against a strong westerly wind and running short of petrol!'

'Short of petrol? Why, how long does this show last?'

'About four hours from start to finish. More if there's anything worth seeing at Valenciennes. But you don't want to waste time there—the Archie can be pretty nasty and there's yet another aerodrome nearby.'

'Altogether an unattractive business,' concluded Wilhelm, as we bent over the map. Rare Earths chuckled again. Valenciennes, I could see, lay some forty miles on the wrong side of the lines. I looked up at my tormentor.

'What's the answer to your question? What *does* one do if there's trouble at the far end of the reconnaissance?'

Rare Earths rubbed his hands together with fiendish glee.

'God knows, my dear fellow! But you'll probably find out in a week's time when you go there yourself. I should say the best thing to do would be to turn east, due east and land in that big forest there'—indicating a green patch on the map—'then you might escape from the angry Germans looking for you. What are you laughing at? You don't think I'm serious? Let me tell you: the first fellow who went on this show was shot down; next time they sent two, one came back; then they sent three, and none of them returned!'

I stood silent.

'What you might call the Law of Diminishing Returns,' murmured Wilhelm.

Rare Earths laughed diabolically and went off to bottle
some samples of Flanders mud which he was taking home
for his collection.

XXIX

Foxy kept very quiet at dinner that night and I noticed
that the major scarcely spoke a word to him. The rumoured
trouble seemed to have some foundation in fact. Afterwards,
while the other members of the mess gradually dispersed,
some to their cabins, some to take a stroll along the river-
bank, others to disappear into holes in the ground (I must
suppose that, for I could never make out where they all went
to), Wilhelm and I lingered over a glass of port, to chat and
also to listen to Foxy. As soon as the major was gone, he
opened up and became his normal self again.

'Yes, I'm leaving,' we heard him tell his friend M.C.
'What happened? Oh, the silliest thing imaginable. No
one but this old Starched Shirt would have made such a fuss
about it. You see, the wing-commander turned up here
before nine o'clock yesterday and saw me going round
the flight with pyjamas on under my coat. Nothing wrong
with that. We shan't lose the war because of it. It was my
morning in bed, no dawn patrol. But of course the major
has to kick up an awful lot of dust. He has thought up
everything he can against me and written to the wing about
it. Net result, I'm to be sent away from the squadron. All
the major's worrying about is himself. He's scared to death
of missing a chance of promotion. . . .'

'Well, what's going to happen to you now?' we heard
M.C. enquire solicitously.

'Oh, I'm all right,' Foxy answered confidently. 'Right
as rain. I'm being sent straight back to England. And I
know plenty of people who will see me through, senior
officers. Probably get my squadron shortly. After all, I'm a
regular officer, and I learnt to fly long before the war; I'm
about due for promotion. But I must say it will be funny
going aboard the boat at Boulogne—remember that fellow
who stands at the head of the gangway? Everyone who
passes he asks: "Leave or duty, sir?" Remember him? Well,

I can't answer that I'm on leave, nor that I'm on duty. I shall have to say that I'm in disgrace. *Tee-hee.* "Leave or duty, sir?"—"Neither. Disgrace!" *Tee-hee-hee!'*

Noticing that Wilhelm and I were tittering with amusement he turned to smile at us benignly.

'Ah, I feel sorry for you young chaps,' he exclaimed with mock compassion. 'Awfully sorry. I'm afraid you'll end by going west. A dud engine or a Fokker on your tail will see the last of you. That Long Reconnaissance—makes me go all goosey to think of it! I hope you'll remember me when I'm gone. There I shall be, with a foot on the rail of the Aero Club bar, drinking something long and strong, and you poor blokes will be freezing stiff over Douai. Then, when I'm sitting in the Piccadilly Restaurant with a steak cooking over the silver grill, I shall pick up a paper and read that you've been brought down and are feeding *behind* the grill in Potsdam! Brr—poor fellows! "Leave or duty, sir?"—"Neither. Disgrace!" *Tee-hee-hee. . . .'*

And so he passed on; and such was his self-assurance that I dare say the trumpets sounded for him on the other side of the Channel.

XXX

The leaves had fallen from the poplars by the river. Gaunt branches pointed to the bleak heavens like a row of upturned brooms. No more did lovers stroll along the towpath at nightfall; they stayed at home in Merville or Estaire, for the nights were cold. The reeds had withered on the bank near the barge whose decks were slippery in the mornings with frost, and the mud in front of the sheds crackled underfoot. Each day seemed scarcely to have dawned before it was already afternoon when pale mists arose to narrow the horizon. Over the quiet landscape the smoke of burning brushwood drifted to mingle its scent with the perfume of damp soil.

And with the dying of the year which had seen the death of so many hopes, there came to this corner of France a mournful yet disquieting hush. All day long the boom of guns shook the air: but now at widely spaced intervals, they

were like the minute-guns of an interminable military
funeral, sounding the knell for an ever-lengthening list of
slain. Even the moan of shells was diminished as though
they moved more slowly through the air; if occasionally
an explosion was louder it was because of the hardness of
partly frozen ground. At night, when the guns were almost
silent, star-shells popped into the sky, hung drowsily swinging, descended glaring evilly at the tired earth. But their
light was now no brighter than the white sparkle reflected
from frosted ridges in furrowed fields or from tufts of grass
beside the Lys. And the rifle fire coming out of the darkness
was scattered and faltering as though the wakeful men in
the trenches, accustomed to nightly alarms, could not be
bothered to reply more warmly. On the ground the air struck
chill, above the treetops it pierced through leather clothing.

An early winter. The first flakes fell. Then came the first
blizzard. On the morning of our Long Reconnaissance the
ground was white with an inch of snow.

'This *is* a ghastly life,' Wilhelm had said the night before.
But in the morning he added: 'I'm glad we're going on this
rotten show. We've been too much like spectators lately.'

XXXI

We started off in fine style. Wilhelm was the first away,
for his was the machine that was to do the reconnaissance,
mine was to provide escort defending him against attack.
Vying with one another to see whose machine could climb
fastest, we made a wide sweep to the west and south whilst
gaining height for the serious work of the day.

I was rather proud of my machine. It was slightly newer
than Wilhelm's and could put up a remarkably good performance. We so rarely flew in company, formation flying
being unknown, that I relished the opportunity of showing
off its powers. After one or two bursts of speed during which
I managed to make up for my later start, I opened the
throttle fully, pushed the nose down to obtain a few more
miles an hour, and then 'zoomed' high over Wilhelm's
head, maintaining the steep climb until my B.E. was on the

verge of stalling. Then I levelled off and looked back. I
had succeeded even better than I had calculated; the other
machine was outdistanced, outclimbed. Wilhelm had vanished.

I must have been singularly blind that day, because at
the time he cannot have been so very far away, but search
as I might I simply could not find him. Turning the machine, throttling the engine to return to his level, banking
hastily from one side to the other, I searched for him everywhere—save, it seems, in the right direction. It was as though
his machine had exploded, been dissipated in fragments as
impalpable as the thin mist rising from the ground. It was,
of course, possible that during my foolish stunting he had
made a vertical turn and dived for home—owing to engine
trouble, or for some other cause—but I did not think it
likely; I felt instinctively sure that he had gone on.

It was a bright sunny morning, although a few wisps of
windblown cloud, mist from the melting snow on the hills
and the glare of the sun in the east made it hard to see. Yet
in the distance, beyond the lines, I fancied at length that
I could discern a speck of an aeroplane. If that were Wilhelm
I must hurry after him, for on the return journey when the
Fokkers came up from Douai he might need my help. At all
events I could not risk letting him down by turning back; it
was my fault that we had become separated. Moreover, we
had orders that if the first machine were forced to abandon
the flight the escort was, if possible, to carry on with the work.
At nine thousand feet (and still climbing) I turned east and
headed for Douai.

Nothing much happened. I don't quite know what I had
been expecting, but whatever it was it did not occur. The
flight was as dull as any I had been on, made no pleasanter
by the fact that I was insufficiently clothed and that it was
freezing hard. Even the country over which we passed offered few features of interest, although it was a little mys-
terious-looking beneath that thin white drapery of snow
through which points of earth appeared jet black like rocks
washed by the foam of a receding tide. The towns, with
firmly pencilled outlines and close-packed roofs gleaming
with moisture, were lustrous. Staring down at them, it was
as though we were gazing into the enemy's soul—a soul

however with remarkably few secrets to tell. There was hardly any movement in the towns, on the roads outside or on the railways. There was not even much Archie.

Rapidly, with an occasional turn or two to give the observer a clear view, we flew over the three main points: Douai, Denain, Valenciennes. At the last place we circled for a few minutes whilst I searched around for the invisible Wilhelm, and the observer hung out over the side of the fuselage to peer down at the network of railway lines, count the rolling-stock and make awkward notes on crumpled, fluttering sheets of paper. My hands and feet were numb and I was shivering uncontrollably when at length we turned homewards.

As there were still no signs of Wilhelm (I learned afterwards that, finding the wind too strong, he had turned back on a northerly course after passing Denain) I decided to take the shortest way home. From a little to the south of Valenciennes we made for Arras, avoiding the perils of Douai. Rubbing hands and knees violently for warmth, I watched the course we followed above the ground, noticing to my annoyance that the top of the compass had frosted over and that however much I tried I could not clear the glass. Luckily there were no clouds or steering might have become difficult. But now we encountered an oft-experienced trouble of these distant flights; the prevailing westerly wind had risen considerably since our departure from the squadron and at ten thousand feet was blowing with great strength. From observation of the ground I estimated that we could be making no more than twenty-five miles an hour against it. At so low a ground-speed we were becoming an easy target for Archie, and we also risked running short of petrol before we could get home. We had to gain speed by losing height. At something not far from eighty miles an hour air-speed we hustled on, descending gradually, engine—of course—full out.

That last was another of the troubles of the Long Reconnaissance. The engine had to be used at full throttle almost all the time if one was to attain the necessary height, carry out the full programme of work and maintain sufficient speed to dodge Archie and enemy aircraft back to the lines, and this left a very small margin of either fuel or engine power if it came to a scrap at the latter end of the journey. Not only the overwhelming Fokkers had forced pilots to come down in enemy territory.

On that day, by way of a change, Archie was extremely inaccurate. But it was not for want of trying. The poor gunners must have given themselves stiff necks staring up at us to watch their bursting shells. And since we were moving so slowly I felt uncomfortably certain that their aim must soon improve. Only a few scattered and spent fragments, however, came near enough to tear small holes in the wings, and but slight deviation was necessary to disturb the poor marksmanship. It was for me the least alarming day of anti-aircraft fire, although I had never seen such heavy or pro-longed shooting. When we were close enough to the lines so that if necessary we could glide to safety without engine power, I turned to look at the shell-bursts behind us. All the way from Valenciennes, hidden now by the haze of distance, to Arras, nearly beneath, the face of the sky was disfigured by a rash of black spots. I made an effort to count them; it was as usual quite hopeless, but in one cluster alone there were ten puffs of smoke. At least a dozen similar clusters could be seen distinctly while many other bursts had already faded: in addition those shells fired at us upon the outward journey had to be reckoned. At a rough guess therefore upwards of two hundred shells must have been fired in the course of a single morning—and not so much as a decent splinter by way of souvenir!

XXXII

But the morning was not over yet. As we reached the trenchlines where they curved about the eastern side of the town of Arras, I saw Archie bursts to the north-west. Our own fellows were hard at their equally unprofitable task. German aircraft were across the lines.

We spotted them almost at once—a couple of grey-blue two-seaters of a type I couldn't recognise—a mile or two away from the nearest Archie. With the engine at full throttle once more, we climbed towards them and almost immediately one of them turned back to the lines at speed, easily outdistancing us and firing a few rounds as he went. The second machine, although a little higher, could not get away so simply. By holding to our course we were bound to intercept him. At last, I thought, we would fight above our own territory.

For an instant, as our two machines drew near, the enemy disappeared behind my own top plane, and the first indication we received that he had turned straight towards us was when a sharp burst of machine-gun fire came spattering past our heads. Then he reappeared above us, still turning, trying to pass over us to reach the lines. My observer opened fire at once from the rear mounting, but an instant later the gun had to be changed. In response to my frantic waving he juggled it into the central 'candlestick' mounting. I had decided that since the enemy was above us I would try to remain underneath and just astern, so that the observer could aim over the top of the propeller. It was a difficult shot, but a good one if I could maintain the position.

Meanwhile the enemy continued to turn; from his observer's comfortable back seat I saw the gun spitting fire that fortunately did no more than hole the wings. But although I conformed to his circling it was some time before we could get in a decent shot in reply. Then with the nose down we had, for a few seconds, a clear field of fire and the observer let off about twenty rounds. At once the enemy turned away and began to dive.

Convinced that we had hit him, I looked hopefully over the side. And again I was disappointed. The enemy's latest turn was aided by the strong westerly wind, carrying us both swiftly across the lines. However badly damaged— and from a faint trail of oily blue smoke I fancied his engine was hit—he was going to get safely home. Taking the risk of running the engine to pieces by giving her full throttle, we dived after him. Archie opened up, trying to intercept us; we ignored him. Over the top of the propeller the observer kept up short steady bursts of fire. The enemy replied intermittently....

We had to give up in the end. By the time my observer had finished his drum of cartridges the enemy had ceased fire. But now with growing anxiety I began to discern the outline of Douai aerodrome, less than two miles ahead. I could see the sheds on the aerodrome, machines waiting in the open.

The necessity for caution came to me suddenly. Fuel was running short, back at the squadron we were already overdue. Abruptly I swung the machine round, headed for home. No use climbing to safety; with the engine at half throttle to save petrol, we flew back nose down, trying to forget the uncomfortable proximity of ever-faithful Archie.

XXXIII

Even now I feel the need to excuse the ending of that flight. By the time we reached the aerodrome beside the Lys we had been in the air for well over four hours during the greater part of which my hands and feet had been more or less frozen. Much staring over the side at the moist shining earth or up at the glare of white clouds had tired my eyes; perhaps, too, the excitement of the fight had been something of a strain. Near Lens, we had run into a snow-storm, adding to our other worries the difficulty of finding the way. And when at length we sighted the aerodrome I dared not circle it lest what I supposed to be the last remaining drops of petrol should give out. Turning into wind I came in to land at once.

The wind blowing in violent gusts made it bumpy in the extreme. The machine rose, fell and swerved beneath me like a small boat in a tide-rip. Were I to let her approach stalling point she would pancake down with the weight of many tons, so that it seemed essential to land fairly fast for I could scarcely feel the controls. Never had that curving little strip of an aerodrome looked so uninviting for a difficult landing; never had the wind blown so erratically, it seemed to come from all directions at once. I landed as best I could, bounced rather badly, and then just as everything was beginning to come right a puff of wind caught the tail, swinging us around. For a few yards we jolted heavily over uneven ground whilst I kicked vainly at the rudder bar; then, slowing down just too late, we rolled into a mound of earth by the riverside. The machine tilted sharply forward—and came to a stop, nose down, propeller smashed. . . . In the distance a shell exploded, but the sound was much less emphatic than my curse.

XXXIV

As hot with shame I struggled out of the cockpit, elevated by the crash to the height of the driver's seat in a hansom cab, I saw to my horror that from the sheds the major was observing me. A group of officers stood about him. I could imagine what they were all saying; and I could imagine that some of them were delighted. Hitherto I had been rather pleased with myself as a pilot, dangerously pleased; they were justly gratified at my humiliation.

I jumped down quickly enough, but my feet were so numb that I had to sit on the mound which had caused my downfall and pull off my flying-boots before I could walk. Meanwhile the observer, who had been free to stamp back circulation during the flight, came valiantly to my rescue. Catching sight of Growl approaching ahead of the others, he marched up to him and presently I heard fragments of his rapid explanation: 'Four hours in the air . . . freezing cold . . . a fight . . . two enemy machines . . . bumpy . . . snowstorm . . .' By the time Growl reached me the venom had gone out of his glance, and after a sarcastic comment on the state of the B.E. he listened calmly to my account of the accident. At the end he became quite friendly.

'Well, young fellow, I suppose you couldn't help it. We all of us crash sometimes, and it might have been worse. Trouble is the wing-commander's here.'

Swinging round to face this new terror I saw the major coming up like an angry ostrich, stepping high and pecking his head at each long stride. At his side was a round little man with a monocle. The wing-commander! Others followed like mutes at a well-attended funeral. I saluted bravely, but no one took any notice of me; all eyes were upon the wrecked machine and the silence was grim with displeasure. In my ears there tingled suddenly a sinister echo: 'Leave or duty? Neither—Disgrace!'

Growl, who was a fearless sort of fellow, forced his way without hesitation into the august presence and began to

give, as if it were his own, my explanation of how everything had happened. The major listened with apparent interest, even going so far as to ask a few questions in a hushed
voice, but the wing-commander had already wandered off
and was bending down to gaze under and into the aeroplane
as though he had never seen one before. When Growl had
stopped speaking, the major went to join him. The wing-
commander's words were borne to me upon the wind: he
had a thin, nasal voice.

'Tell me, what did the pilot—er—want to crash for?'

I thought that never in my life had I heard such a stupid
question. But I blessed the major for his answer.

'Oh, he was in the air for a very long time, Valenciennes
and back. And he had the very devil of a scrap—chased a
German all the way to Douai, made him land!'

At that moment I felt genuine affection for my commanding-officer. It was the first time in my experience that he had
seemed really human. And his words had their effect. The
wing-commander opened his eyes. The monocle fell out. It
had not been known to do so within the memory of living
man.

.   .   .   .   .

'What did the Starched Shirt say to you?' one of the pilots
asked me when the crowd about my machine had dispersed a
little. I told him that at present I considered the major one
of the best and kindest of men. Had he not spoken up for me
to the wing-commander?

'And so he jolly well ought to,' was the reply. 'After all,
he takes what credit he can for work done by the squadron,
and you get the blame for crashing. . . .'

But on this occasion I argued the Starched Shirt's case
with heat.

Near the sheds later on, M.C. accosted me.

'Damn' bad luck, that landing of yours. This aerodrome
is simply impossible when the wind blows across. . . . Hear
you had a fight. With two of them? How did it go?'

I was amazed. He was interested. His tone was warm,
friendly. I wondered if I had misjudged him.

On the way to make out a report of the morning's doings,

I found Wilhelm completing his. We compared notes as to where we had been and how I had managed to miss him at the start of the reconnaissance. He wanted to know all about the fight.

'By the way,' he exclaimed at length, 'that's four fights you've had now—you're level with me and ahead of anyone else in the squadron. Better stop for a while or I'll be getting jealous! But, I say, I am sorry to hear you crashed. Rotten luck!'

Four hours in the air may not seem very long nowadays, although in a draughty B.E. in winter, it could be tiring enough. But it occurred to me that I should not have attracted so much friendly attention had I made a perfect landing at the end of it.

XXXV

I was not, I soon discovered, in disgrace, and yet I could not help feeling that it was on my account the wing-commander did not stop to lunch. But then visitors very rarely did stay to lunch, in fact they seldon came into the mess at all. Perhaps they sensed from afar the gloom, the chilly silences, the petty ill-feeling that disunited us. One could not blame visitors for looking at their wrist-watches and murmuring must-get-back, lot-of-work-to-do excuses. I sometimes felt I would like to go with them; the trenches must be warm and cheery compared to our dank inhospitable barge.

One day a general did come to lunch with us. His name was 'Boom'* because of his voice, but we were not privileged to hear more than a word or two of it. Save to put food in, he scarcely opened his mouth during the whole uncomfortable meal. The major kept up a droning monologue, like a country parson incanting the Litany, in a voice barely audible above the guarded clatter of knives and forks. Otherwise no one spoke except to ask for the bread, the butter or the salt, please. We all drank water.

Immediately after lunch Boom disappeared and we saw him no more. In the morning we had felt very nervous at the thought of his coming, of what his keen eyes would see, of

* Trenchard.

whether he would quietly approve or thunder forth his stern condemnation. When he had gone we were disappointed that he had not inspected, that he had not spoken to us personally, individually. A word from him would have been encouraging. A pity he, too, was so aloof. It made his visit seem rather uninspiring. And somehow it confirmed my suspicion that we were neither popular nor interesting. In fact, we were not a good squadron; not a bad lot, only young, dull and very ill-assorted.

XXXVI

I was beginning to like Growl, possibly because he was beginning to like me. With his neat canvas leggings, hands thrust into the front pockets of his riding-breeches, coat flaps pushed back behind his wrists, feet firmly planted well apart, he had the appearance—enhanced by his clean-shaven, weather-beaten face, by a straw between his teeth, and by that gruff voice which could change so rapidly from wrath to good-humour—of something between a horse-dealer and a buccaneer. At times I would catch him looking at me with an expression, half frown, half smile, such as a pirate skipper might bestow upon a likely lad. It was a pity that he was never able to give me any hints as to how to fight the enemy in the air, but in those days each man had to learn and progress from his own experience and, as luck would have it, I was gaining mine quicker than most—too quickly perhaps.

'Do you know anything about bomb-sights?' he asked me one day.

'Not a thing,' I admitted. 'I've never even seen one.'

'Then, young fellow, you had better hurry and find out all you can. The mechanics are fitting bomb-racks to your machine. . . . Hey! Where are you going?'

'To stop them before it's too late.'

'No use!' he exclaimed with a malicious chuckle. 'The job's more than half-done. Tomorrow you're to practise with the sight over the aerodrome near Béthune. And the day after that you and a lot of enthusiastic young pilots will go a-bombing.'

I protested that one day's practice would not be sufficient to teach me to hit any target with certainty.

'Never mind, young fellow, you do what your elders and betters think is good for you. You'll have plenty of company on the raid. Rare Earths is going with you; and M.C. will be among the escort. Several other squadrons are competing —something like twenty-five machines in all, each carrying two 112-pound bombs. That makes two and a half tons, on one railway junction—you ought to do *some* damage even if you miss the target altogether!'

Put like that, the raid seemed to offer immense possibilities. Excitedly I asked if the war were starting again. But at that Growl only laughed and told me not to be silly. He went on leave that same afternoon.

XXXVII

No sooner had I tried the bomb-sight in the air than I realised that it would be utterly impossible for me to learn to use it in under two days' time. A rather complicated apparatus, it required some skill and experience in the using. Above all it required two flights over the target; the first one to get the wind's speed and direction and to make sundry calculations with a stop-watch and notebook, the second flight to drop the bombs. Since observers had to be dispensed with owing to the added weight of bombs, all the calculations had to be done by the pilot. I did not fancy myself sitting above an angry Archie battery and scratching my head over a complicated sum in arithmetic, especially if the final result was to be the totally inaccurate placing of my bombs. The more I thought of it the less the prospect pleased me.

On the day of the raid I came to a decision. I said nothing to anyone, for Growl and Wilhelm were both on leave, but I made up my mind that if, after an attempt to aim my first bomb by means of the sight, I missed the target I would descend to a much lower level than was prescribed and deposit the second bomb exactly where I wanted it. When, at the last moment, I learned that we were to make two trips each, dropping four bombs apiece, I felt certain of achieving something by my own methods. It meant disobeying orders and

taking extra risk, but I had some small confidence in myself
and none in the sight.

The meet, at which our B.E.s supplied both the pack and
the field, was timed for 11 a.m., and we were due to move off
a quarter of an hour later from the neighbourhood of
Béthune. Arriving punctually, I found three or four machines
circling around; two more turned up from my own squadron,
and between Béthune and the lines there were a few others.
But there was nothing like the important gathering I had been
told to expect. People coming from squadrons far to the
north had apparently decided to cut the meet altogether; I
could see isolated machines in the distance already being
archied. Waiting no longer, I gave my machine her head and
jogged off to the railway junction at Don, from which if we
could not actually draw a fox, we might at least hope to tempt
a Fokker.

There was, of course, no question of formation—that
additional peril to flying had not yet been invented. Machines
arrived when they liked, dropped their bombs and dashed
home to lunch. But the sight if not spectacular was at all
events rather impressive, with a score of aeroplanes scattered
over the sky and many dozens of Archie bursts even more
scattered. One advantage of do-as-you-please and no-
formation was that Archie never quite knew at which machine he was aiming. Every one of us was at a different
altitude, dodging in his own peculiar way and in his own good
time. All the puzzled anti-aircraft gunners could do was to
fire into the brown, hoping that the odd fragment might
score a hit. And by the laws of chance it sometimes did; but
not very often.

The wind was from the north, and on the south side of
the junction a collection of machines assembled, each waiting
its turn to fly into wind over the target. The crowd did not
look any too safe to me; as if the field were hung up, bunched
in front of the only gap over a dangerous jump. Machines
were jostling each other in their anxiety to get ahead and
have done with the job, and to add to the confusion Archie,
without doing any real harm, was beginning to find the range.
At from nine to ten thousand feet—the height at which the
raid took place—Archie was considered to be fairly innocu-
ous, but I noticed that, despite the conscientious way in

which some machines were circling twice over the target to adjust sights before dropping their bombs, he was putting them off their aim: a good many misses were being registered in the fields at the side of the railway track. I should do no better if I joined the crowd; I should only get in their way and in the way of Archie. I must strike out on my own, lower down, much lower.

To dive towards the railway with the engine at half-throttle was easy enough, but on the way the thought occurred to me that I might now get hit by one of the bombs from the machines above. The chance of this happening was no greater than of being hit by an unexploded Archie shell, yet the idea so alarmed me that I decided at once not to go round twice adjusting the sight, but to drop the bombs quickly by luck and judgment. For this it did not seem worth while going below two thousand feet, where ground machine-gunners were adding to the racket. Approaching the junction with the engine still throttled down I could also hear the uneven popping and crackling of rifle fire—heavier than usual, it seemed. Peering over the side, I could at first see nothing to warrant so much noise. The railway station was a bit knocked about and appeared to be deserted, but a short distance out of it, on a curve well away from the junction a train was standing motionless, the engine blowing off steam. Beside it there were many agitated black dots. . . . A troop train! The men had disembarked and it was from them that the rifle fire was coming. To use the sight now was out of the question; my one idea was to get rid of the two bombs without delay. No time to waste; I pulled both release handles. The bombs dropped off.

Watching closely, I followed them down to the ground . . . Both missed the station—of course! The first one fell in a roadway not far from a level-crossing, but far enough to be quite harmless. A flash and a big puff of smoke from the second bomb appeared in the courtyard of a house twenty yards from the railway line and about two hundred yards from the station. My aim—from which I had expected such wonderful results—had proved to be hopeless. And yet in that courtyard where the second bomb exploded I saw motor-transport, and the smoke which hung over the place afterwards seemed to indicate that something had been set on fire.

Better than nothing. But I wished that I had been given a few more bombs to practise with; half a dozen more and I *might* have hit the station itself.

Now that it was all over I felt very disappointed. It was a pity I had come down so low to achieve so meagre a result, whilst high above in the sky I could see a couple of Fokkers and a German two-seater with whom I might have had a more profitable engagement. M.C., I imagined, must be having a grand time.

On the way home, no sooner had I got clear of the worst of Archie than I flew into a snowstorm which, while it lasted, was so much more terrifying than anything the enemy had done that when at length I landed at the squadron, with the machine coated with ice, my account of the morning's work was incoherent.

XXXVIII

For once everybody in the mess was talking at the same time. The three or four pilots who had been bombing had returned before me and were eagerly discussing the results, and I noted with embarrassment that they all claimed to have obtained direct hits on the station. The others, like M.C., who had acted as escort were commenting on the fights they had had and on whatever they had been able to see of the bombing. The major went from one to the other like an interested spectator after a football match, asking questions, faintly smiling, showing keenness, almost excitement, but unable to get a word in above the unwonted tumult. A few more shows like this, I thought, and he would become an enthusiast in spite of himself. It had made us all keener. If the raid had not been an unqualified success, at least it had given us something to do, something of an offensive sort against the enemy to lighten the gloom of winter. I was relieved, however, that my own answers to questions vaguely and hurriedly put were hardly listened to.

'Did you see that barge sink in the canal alongside the station?' someone asked, addressing the crowd in general. 'A bomb fell right inside it, direct hit—it sank like a stone!'

'Yes, I saw that,' someone else replied. 'But it seemed to

me that it blew up before it sank—must have had ammunition on board. Personally I aimed at that train standing on
the curve. Think I got a direct hit—knocked out some of
the troops.'

The major was murmuring, 'Well done, well done,' whilst
at my side M.C. was speaking.

'Archie *was* busy, wasn't he? Sending up a lot of those
"Flaming Onions", too—nasty things, but they didn't do
any good. I suppose the gunners were afraid of hitting their
own side—quite a few enemy aircraft about. Did anyone
see those two Fokkers?'

We answered in chorus. Everyone had seen them, some
had tried to fight them.

'I thought one of them was going to dive on me,' someone
said. 'But I fancy there were too many of us to make it
attractive.'

'I chased one for a mile or two,' M.C. went on. 'I couldn't
get near enough to shoot, so I came back to watch the
bombing. It looked as though the station had been pretty
badly hit.'

Suddenly he stuck out his jaw, glaring around in emulation
of Growl's best pirate-captain manner.

'Who the devil was that silly ass flying at about two
thousand feet, collecting all the machine-gun fire? Who was
it?'

XXXIX

At noon I was weak with hunger, for which I ate a hearty
lunch. Afterwards I was weak with indigestion, for which I
took a large glass of brandy. After the brandy I felt mildly
intoxicated, for which the only remedy appeared to be to
leave the ground as quickly as possible. Scrambling into the
B.E. I steamed hilariously away with two nice new bombs
hooked up underneath.

Over Don other aeroplanes were returning one by one
from the luncheon interval, but there was not the same
dangerous crush as in the morning. Not that it would have
worried me in the least had the crowd been twice as thick.
I was in no mood for dallying. Now that the ice was broken

—in a manner of speaking, for it was still freezing hard in the air—I intended to pursue the same tactics as earlier in the day, but more boldly. An easterly breeze had blown the snowstorm out of the sky, the air was crisp, the weather wintry but fine. I wished that I had with me that cavalry observer; I felt like making huntin' noises. Everything seemed favourable to the attack; even Archie kept a friendly distance, encouraging me with an occasional cough well above my head as I dived Don-wards.

There could be no doubt about my judgment this time. If *in vino veritas* has any meaning, it meant just then that I was an extremely fine dropper of bombs. I don't want to exaggerate to my own detriment the effect of the spirit I had drunk, but it must have been Napoleon brandy—I had the eye of an eagle; damn it, I felt like an eagle! An eagle laying high-explosive eggs. . . . Long before reaching the site I saw black dots moving. German dots: '*Entschuldigen sie bitte, meine Herren,*' I murmured and pulled the first release handle.

I was sure of having pulled it too soon; the bomb would fall so far from its mark that the very sound of the explosion would be inaudible in Don. And then I saw a flash in a big building between the station and the canal, débris flew high and wide, a column of smoke shot upwards. It was rather satisfying. I circled round quickly for the second shot. Near the station more black dots were moving. '*Bitte, meine Herren, ruhig bleiben. Es kommt noch eine ...*' I watched the bomb go down, diminishing rapidly to a pinpoint, then suddenly expanding again as it struck a building in the goods yard. A flash, bricks and dust, and lots of slow-spreading smoke . . . I flew home, humming a tune.

Twenty aeroplanes—two bombs each, two trips each— four tons of bombs upon one small railway junction. The biggest raid the Flying Corps had yet carried out. . . . At the squadron office we wrote our reports feverishly, anxious to know what would happen next.

Next? Well, the excitement died down. The reports went in and were filed. Aerial photographs were taken of the damage done. Press *communiqués* mentioned the raid cautiously, observing that similar bombardments had preceded the battles of Neuve-Chappelle and Loos. But the opposing armies made no move. The incident seemed to have no meaning or value in the main trend of the war. It was soon forgotten. An extra number of star-shells lit up the country-side for a night or two; there was a little more rifle fire than usual; the enemy was nervous. Nothing else.

Nowadays when I recall Don Junction, which is not often, it is to wonder how many luckless French civilians were in or about the station whilst we flew carelessly overhead thinking it all rather good fun.

XL

The bombing of Don took place upon the 27th of November, and early on the next day an urgent message came through from the watchful anti-aircraft batteries in our neighbourhood announcing that the lines had been crossed by a number of enemy aeroplanes. The squadron came to life. M.C. and Rare Earths made ready their respective machines. My observer came running breathlessly from the barge to the hangar where I was already waiting, with orders for us to leave at once. Quick to obey such a joyful command, we were off the ground before the others.

And almost immediately we sighted an enemy, a big white-winged two-seater Albatross, far above us and flying parallel to the lines, reconnoitring our positions. So far above was he that I doubted if we could ever climb up to his height to catch him before he went home; like most German machines, he had a greater turn of speed than we had.

The chase started over Neuve-Chapelle when we were at two thousand feet and he at about eight thousand. It continued in a straight line as far as Armentières, by which time—the enemy having descended a little—we had drawn nearly level at six or seven thousand. Then to our chagrin he turned eastwards and before we could fire had crossed the lines. Forestalling this turn, expected since the beginning of the pursuit, by keeping well to eastward of him I managed to get ahead, only losing a little in height in gaining the necessary speed. Five miles across the lines, with the machine-gun on the rear mounting, we engaged him.

Strangely enough I do not think that until the instant when we opened fire he had been aware of our presence. Probably he had been intent on gazing to the west, giving only an occasional glance to the east where, with the sun in his eyes, the B.E. had remained almost invisible. Thinking himself safe, he throttled down to glide towards Lille; and passed within twenty yards of our starboard wing-tips. . . .

Twenty or thirty rounds my observer fired, not more, then, as the enemy turned across our bows, ceased fire to change the gun to the forward mounting.

I had expected to hear heavy fire from the enemy's back seat, for, while the gun was being changed and as we started to dive after him, he had an easy chance to get us. But to my astonishment not a shot came in answer. When the gun was ready the observer gave him another burst, a very short one because the Albatross was turning faster, gliding more steeply. His glide was becoming a dive; a dive at so steep an angle that I could no longer make the B.E. follow. And the turn he was making now had something unnatural about it—he was going down out of control! For a moment we both watched, fascinated.

A sudden crack of bullets made us swing our heads round; made the observer jump for the Lewis gun with a movement that shook the machine. Over our heads sailed another Albatross. And even as I banked the B.E. swiftly away from this new danger I saw, returning from the west, two more enemy craft.

Bullets cracked by. Our gun replied with several long bursts, its barrel getting as hot as the observer changing it hastily from one mounting to another. The B.E., jarring from frequent impacts, banked, dodged, dived and zoomed as though she knew what was wanted, accepting all that I could give her from the immense store of my eighty-three hour's flying experience. And while we were firing and wheeling, from out of the skies came a fourth enemy. It seemed as if the curse laid on those who shoot an Albatross had descended upon us.

Four German aeroplanes, one curveting B.E. Even Archie stopped to watch.

XLI

When an hour or so later we returned to the squadron it seemed that at least a week had passed. I felt as though I had not slept for days, although I might have dreamed. The morning was sunny, the air calm. I brought the B.E. down carefully; the wind was in just the right direction, I made a good landing. As the machine came to rest in front of the hangars I remember calling out to the observer, in the sudden silence after the stopping of the engine, 'Well done—good show!' And so it had been; swinging that gun around from mounting to mounting, hanging on whilst I did the wildest of turns, keeping a cool head in an emergency, demanded from the observer the qualities of an acrobat, a strong man, and a juggler. And whereas his many bursts of fire had eventually driven off the whole pack of enemies, his first few rounds had been accurate, deadly. No doubt of that; the enemy had gone down and crashed. Ten miles inside his own lines, but crashed nevertheless. A satisfactory, almost an unhoped for, result; previous to this fight I had begun to doubt the possibility of ever bringing down an enemy until we were better equipped. I had been reminded of that Cautionary Tale in which Algernon, playing with a loaded gun:

'. . . pointed it towards his sister,
Aimed very carefully, but missed her.'

It had seemed that we were destined always to aim very carefully, but miss the enemy. At last we had aimed and hit. 'Well done!' I repeated.

The observer turned to look at me with open mouth and raised eyebrows as though he did not quite understand.

'Good shooting on your part,' I said. 'Just one big burst and down he went.'

His brows were still raised in surprise. 'Did he *really* go down?' he asked at length. 'I *thought* I saw him dive out of control, but I wasn't sure—it all seemed so unreal. Good thing you kept dodging—I couldn't move that gun any quicker, my hands are still numb from hauling it around. I suppose it *must* have been real!'

I laughed at his doubts, though I was not far from sharing them. Aerial fighting, more than any other, seems so immensely far away when one stands once more on the earth, with the machine-guns silent, the engine still, the sky empty.

'Come and look at the damage,' I said. 'That's real enough.'

It was not so much the quantity of hits as the quality of the damage done. One of the interplane struts was shot through, a rudder control cable cut away, the air-speed indicator smashed, the propeller chipped, a longeron in the fuselage pierced and splintered (that last bullet had grazed the back of my seat)—twenty hits altogether. But we had won something of a victory. Later on *The Times*, meaning to be kind, described it as a 'gallant fight against odds', as if the odds had been of our choosing! As for 'gallant'— well, one of its meanings is courteous, and that the fight was —at least for a moment or two. A sharp turn to avoid one enemy had brought us close alongside another, dangerously close, within pistol shot. Our own gun was momentarily out of action, between mountings, and we could see the enemy observer working over his as though reloading or clearing a jam. We were actually close enough to see the expression upon each other's faces, but powerless to do harm. I don't know yet what came over me, whether nervousness, excitement, or just a fellow-feeling for the man opposite in the same position as myself; but it was at any rate a joyful impulse that made me raise my arm to wave across the narrow air space. And from the gunner's cockpit of that enemy biplane, the German waved back to me. Just a single wave of the arm above his head, a salute as it might have been in the days of tilting, of knights in armour and of wooden lances. Then, his gun being ready, he opened fire. My observer was still loading, I was forced to turn away in self-protection. I had only an automatic pistol, but I discharged it defiantly. . . .

In those days a machine was repaired sooner than scrapped or replaced. It took two days for mechanics working morning, noon, and night to repair my B.E. The day after they had finished I had reason to wish that they had taken longer.

In flight: rivals of 1918. (*above*) S.E.5a (*below*) Fokker D VII

Larry: Lieutenant Laurence G. Bowen RFC
and RAF (American). Killed in action 15

Gilly: Major Euan Gilchrist MC, DFC,
O.C. 56 Squadron RFC and RAF

XLII

In the Koran it is written: 'The fate of every man have we bound about his neck.' The words might well have been painted over the companion of our drab and unromantic barge. For, if I cannot profess to speak for the respective fates of the other officers in the squadron, of the inevitable nature of my own small destiny I have no remaining doubt.

The bombing of Don had roused the German airmen to activity over our territory. Whether they came to see what we were up to or to take reprisals for our raid mattered not, they had to be chased away. In the course of such a chase I had had that fifth and biggest fight in which an enemy machine had been brought down near Lille. In an attempt to confirm the wrecking of this enemy craft, Wilhelm, just back from leave, was sent into the air to locate and photograph it. The enemy, possibly expecting further trouble in the vicinity of Lille, had their Fokkers ready. One of them surprised Wilhelm at his work, outfought him and shot him down —a prisoner and wounded.

The Long Reconnaissance was coming round again. The third flight (the one which did not live on the barge and which enjoyed a measure of independence in a farmhouse) was now wholly occupied in artillery observation; they did no Long Reconnaissance work. The flight which Foxy had commanded had been the last to attempt the job (they had abandoned it owing to bad weather); it was therefore the turn of the flight to which I belonged. But with Wilhelm captured, Growl away on leave and Rare Earths' machine laid up for overhaul, I was the only pilot available: the other flight would have to do the reconnaissance after all. But now they, too, claimed that they were short of machines and pilots, or would be for a few days. Moreover the weather looked as though it might remain unsuitable for a week and at the end of that time the Long Reconnaissance duty would lapse, passing to another squadron. The flight that had been Foxy's was quite willing for this to happen because only M.C.'s machine was ready to take the air.

Growl was returning from leave in a day's time. During his absence we had done a lot of good work. Patrols, reconnaissances, the bombing raid; we had had the big fight; but

E

we had lost Wilhelm. It would be a great thing, I thought, if we could produce the achievement of a successful Long Reconnaissance with which to greet him on his arrival. The result of the big fight had brought me some small *kudos,* but it was clear that to please the major I should have to keep up the good work and not rest upon whatever swiftly fading laurels I might have earned. The day before the reconnaissance was due I made up my mind.

With all the insane enthusiasm of improvident youth I volunteered to go, with M.C. as escort. Till then only a slender concatenation of circumstances had led me forward, but from the moment when I made my choice the chain was finally welded. I had tempted fortune too far.

XLIII

Still rather dejected by the loss of Wilhelm and his observer, we were nevertheless an unusually jolly party in the mess on the night before I went on my second Long Reconsaissance. And the reason was not far to seek. The major was dining and sleeping at headquarters, Growl was in England, Foxy was in 'disgrace'; with the possible exception of M.C., the entire range of cats was away and the mice therefore put up a bold squeaking. Even so there were too few in the mess to make a really cheerful din.

'This squadron *is* getting small,' a young pilot remarked, looking round the table. 'Hardly enough of us to do the work! Wish they'd send some more out from England.'

One of the observers gave a chuckle.

' "Nay, wish not one man more . . ." ' he quoted.

The young pilot was scornful.

'You imagine the fewer of us the greater the share of honour?' he retorted. 'Balderdash! There's only one man in the squadron liable to come in for any honour—and I don't suppose you'll claim that our old Starched Shirt has the personality of Harry the King. Wonder what he would be like in a real emergency, a tight corner—if the Germans came here, for instance?'

'Not much likelihood of that,' M.C. declared. 'It's much more probable that we shall go and join the Germans. Per-

sonally I think Foxy is well out of it—sent back to England
with nothing against him except a vague complaint about
his pyjamas. Think of him now, sitting in his club or in some
swell restaurant in London, cocktails, dress clothes, carna-
tion in buttonhole, beautiful lady dining with him...' He
broke off to make a pretence of shuddering. 'Brrr—makes
me go all goosey to think of him!'

The observer who was to accompany me on the morrow
grinned.

'Yes, Foxy *will* laugh if we go and dine in Potsdam after
the reco, won't he? What do you think,' he asked me, 'do
you suppose we are scheduled to "go west" tomorrow?'

I shook my head emphatically. Not on my life, I maintained stoutly, would anything so disastrous occur. If we
went at all, and the weather made it uncertain, we would
return just as we had done from a score of previous flights
across the lines. My leave was due at Christmas and on that
day I had every intention of dining at home. I laughed at
his fears.

But I must have forgotten to touch wood.

XLIV

We stood upon the canal bank near the hangars. It was
after breakfast on the following morning.

'Do you think it's good enough?' M.C. asked, looking
doubtfully at the sky.

My observer answered him firmly, resentful of the suggestion behind his words that we should not go at all.

'Certainly it's good enough—to make a start at any rate.
There's not too much wind and there are gaps in the clouds
—look, the sun's coming through!'

They both turned to me. As the actual reconnaissance
pilot my judgment must be final. Avoiding their gaze, I
stared at the clouds and listened to the wind in the poplars.
The waters of the Lys were ruffled; dead leaves whisked
along the towpath, tumbled into the river and sailed up-
stream in crescent formation like a miniature armada. Small
waves broke against the bows of the barge, brushed past
leaving a track of frothy bubbles. The canvas walls of the

hangars billowed steadily for a while with the pressure of air within, then collapsed suddenly against the poles with a dull boom like the sails of a ship taken aback. In front of the sheds stood the two duty aeroplanes, rocking slightly as the breeze caught their wings. From their wires, as from the bare branches of the poplars, came a mournful soughing.

I shivered; the air was cold and damp. . . . How far away the summer of Shoreham and Gosport seemed! Then there would have been no doubt about a day like this; 'unfit for flying' or perhaps 'no lift in the air' would have been the decision. But it was for such weather and such work as this that I had been trained. Orders had been left at the squadron office that the reconnaissance must be made if the weather were at all possible. Could it honestly be termed 'impossible'? I thought not, although I longed now for a definite order to cancel the flight. But Growl was away, the major had not yet returned from headquarters; it was for me to decide. I glanced about, taking in all the signs of the weather.

Mechanics stood by the machines, holding on to the wings. They looked cold, only half awake. Poor fellows, they had a dull life of it; no flights on fine sunny days, no adventure, no aerial combats. But their quarters were hardly less comfortable than ours—better than the trenches!—and they were not called upon to make fateful decisions, to risk 'going west'. . . . A flight-sergeant hovered nearby, keeping an eye on the mechanics, ready to spring to attention when called. M.C. frowned gloomily as if to emphasise his own unfavourable opinion, and the two observers having had their say waited in silence, holding maps and notebooks.

And all these men were watching, I could feel their eyes upon me. They were watching as I blinked up at the sky, watching when I stared at the horizon, watching and waiting for that final verdict which it was mine to give and so direct their immediate actions. I could have stood there all day irresolute—but my observer was right, we must make an attempt.

'Let's go,' I said to M.C. at length. 'I believe we shall find clear weather beyond the lines. We can always turn back if it gets too bad.'

But I was inwardly convinced that, once we got under way,

there would be no returning until we had circled Valenciennes.

My observer led the way to the machine.

'Start up!' the flight-sergeant shouted to the waiting
mechanics. 'Get those engines going. Smartly now!'

The die was cast.

XLV

Down the curving stretch of the aerodrome the wind blew
lustily, lifting us vertically over the trees at the far end.
Holding straight on, I prudently gained height before turning;
it was not a day to risk a landing down wind. At fifteen hundred feet we passed back over the squadron.

The escorting machine with M.C. as pilot was well below
and behind; apparently he had wanted to see me safely
away before taxi-ing out to take off, but I was momentarily
puzzled for there were two B.E.s in the air below me. As
I watched, one of them went down to land, taxied along the
riverside, stopped by our flight sheds. Now that it was on the
ground I could see it was not M.C.'s machine; there was a
newness about the colour of its wings. . . . Growl had returned,
that was it, bringing a machine to replace the one lost with
Wilhelm. He would be pleased, I thought, to see us going off
punctually despite the poor weather. I watched the brown
dot of him striding towards the barge.

The narrow world in which I had dwelt for nearly three
months moved swiftly by. In spite of its restrictions, in spite
of its atmosphere of ill-feeling, of distrust, of envy and of
hidden malice it had taken a friendly, almost a home-like
grip upon me. It was not the fault of one more than another
among us that we were so cheerless and so stiff; it was the
closeness of our confinement in the barge, the small circle of
our daily horizon, the dismal winter futility of the war. With
a little generosity one could afford to absolve the major from
blame, because there can be no doubt that he suffered from
a constitutional disability to inspire comradeship. That he
was willing to meet changing conditions seemed evident from
his having left the gunners for the Flying Corps; and despite
my early prejudice I had found myself liking him at times,

but they certainly did not think much of him in the squadron. He must have sighed with relief when at length he left it. Some time after the war I saw him, dressed in the new blue uniform of the Royal Air Force. He still walked like a melancholy bird. And appropriately enough, considering the circumstances in which I best remembered him, he was judging a competition for landing aeroplanes within a small space. . . .

Although he had been expected back early at the squadron he was not there to see me off when I left on that Long Reconnaissance, and once I had started it made no difference where he was. Even had he and Growl met in anxious conference near the farmhouse where the squadron office was situated, there would have been no means of recalling me. But, Growl gone, the aerodrome remained deserted. The pilots were at breakfast or, profiting from the bad weather and general inactivity, still in bed. The farm buildings and transport lines passed beneath; a hedge, the corner of a ploughed field; then the barge, dirty grey with an untidy deck—I could make out the skylight of the mess, the porthole of my cabin next to it. The Lys, its surface the hue of steel, was curved like a sabre, the edge to the east. The poplars straight as guardsmen on parade became foreshortened, became dots, then rapidly lengthened again. Merville passed under my right wing. The squadron lay astern.

I faced forward to pick out the landmarks on the southerly course to Arras. The machine was climbing rapidly, we were already through the first thin bank of scattered clouds and the trenchlines to the east and south were visible. No one could have called it a fine day, yet it seemed good enough for our purpose. There were heavy clouds above us, but the sun was shining through the upper layers and over German territory the air was clear. If only the westerly wind, against which we should have to struggle on the return journey, did not strengthen. . . . Contrary winds, however, were only to be expected as a part of the day's work; the reconnaissance had to be done.

I looked back once more to check my course and the drift of the wind; but Merville and the aerodrome were obscured by a rain-cloud.

3

The Wings Are Clipped

I

We were nearing ten thousand feet when we approached
Arras from the west, for this time I did not intend to commence work at anything less than that height; I wanted to
be sure of seeing my way clearly above the clouds. Arras
itself was partly hidden, but there were plenty of gaps to
show me the lines, and to the east there was a vast area of
clear sky. That hornets' nest of Douai showed up distinctly,
bright in the wintry sunlight. Hazy in the distance lay the
towns we had to visit. An easy course to steer, only the wind
to worry about.

As we reached the lines I looked back to seek M.C. in
the escorting aeroplane, but he was nowhere in sight. That
he had been with us as far as Lens I knew, I had seen him
several times. Of course it was possible that I had outdistanced him since my machine, I had reason to believe, could
climb faster than his; he might even be hidden from us by
one of the many big cumulus clouds. At all events it seemed
unlikely that he, our escort, should already have turned back.
I waited, making figures of eight above Arras.

Bad weather was coming up from the west, no doubt of
it. If this job were to be done at all, 'twere best done quickly.
. . . Again I searched the sky. No, not a sign of M.C. We were
above ten thousand feet, time was precious, I dared not wait
longer. Heading east we crossed the lines. My observer made
ready his map and notebook; the Long Reconnaissance had
started.

II

Almost at once we sighted a German two-seater. One thousand feet below us, heading north-east to cross the lines. I increased to full speed, losing height so as to get to the eastward of him and drive him towards our own territory: then, signalling to the observer to place the gun on the forward mounting, turned to attack.

There was a flash from the enemy's back-seat gun as he opened fire, but I could not hear the bullets pass; his aim was poor and the range none too close. I pushed the nose down for a further increase of speed, but before my observer could get in a shot the enemy wheeled and went into a dive. A big mountain of a cloud rose up in front of him. He plunged into it, effectively checking our pursuit.

As I glued my eyes to that cloud, watching like a terrier in front of a rat-hole for his reappearance, my gaze fell once more upon the war-scarred town of Arras with the chalk-white line of trenches running through its eastern suburbs. We were recrossing the battle front, back to our own lines. . . . I hesitated. Somewhere in the big cloud was the enemy, trying to elude us. Were we to wait for him and then follow, there would be a long, probably a disappointing chase. We could not hope to surprise him; it was quite on the cards that we should fail to overhaul him. M.C. with his escorting aeroplane might have helped, but he was not in sight. I looked to the east. The open country, clear of clouds, seemed to be inviting our inspection. The Long Reconnaissance was more important than any aerial combat; we had orders not to force an engagement on the way out. On the way back—well, there might yet be plenty of excitement if the Fokkers rose from Douai.

On the far side of the cloud the German two-seater came out of concealment, heading due north. He was travelling fast, the range had already opened a great deal. My observer caught sight of him, pointed enthusiastically. But I shook my head and steered east. The observer replaced the gun upon the rear mounting, brought out his map, rearranged his notebook.

III

Aided by the west wind we made rapid progress. Douai we left a mile or two to the north, time enough to visit it on the return journey if all went well. The principal objective was Valenciennes. I made haste to reach it before the unsettled weather changed for the worse.

In a comparatively short time we were above Denain, where the observer—he was that same Dante of the patrol during the King's visit—Dante, began a feverish taking of notes. Every now and then he would wave one arm or the other to indicate the way I should turn to give him a better view of road or rail, transport or trains, of anything new or unusual to interest the Intelligence people. It was hard for him to see what was happening in the stations for we were now at twelve thousand feet in brilliant sunshine and below us the light was poor, misty. For some ten minutes we cruised around over the town. It was very quiet. Archie sent up three shells.

On to Valenciennes. The wind must be increasing in strength, I thought; the earth passed very swiftly. On the roads and in the country generally, nothing much worth observing other than a train or two in the sidings. And not a machine in the sky, not a speck anywhere, not so much as a shell-burst. Only a threatening bank of clouds to the west.

Valenciennes at last. Still in France, and yet to us it seemed the very heart of the enemy's territory. What unpleasantness were they preparing down there? We went beyond the town for a couple of miles, staring curiously at the mysterious land. A road and a railway led to the east—to Mons! No use in going farther that way; there was nothing doing in that direction now. I turned back to circle the town. The glare had gone from the surface of the ground, the haze had been blown away, the air was clear. We had reached thirteen thousand feet, but above us the sky was clouding over even as Dante hung over the side to count rolling-stock. Not much movement in the big railway station, nothing out of the ordinary; but to the south a long train was winding down the track towards Cambrai, another moved in the direction of Avesnes. I could see that Dante had noticed them and intended to deal with them later; meanwhile he

wanted to have another look at Valenciennes. He waved for
me to circle again.

This time as we turned I observed how almost stationary
we appeared to be when facing west; the wind had risen.
It would be a slow and tiresome business flying back against
it, there were rain or snow clouds on our course; already
it was bitterly cold, my hands were numb. And the top of
the compass was frosted over as on previous chilly occasions
when, in obedience to Dante's waving arm, I turned south,
glad to be off from the neighbourhood. Its silence was uncanny. An old French fort stared up at us like the eye of a
Cyclops. Why didn't Archie fire? Had the gunners not seen
us, or did they think the weather so bad that they need not
add to our difficulties? Perhaps they were right; it was a
stormy day and ours was the only machine in the sky.
Thank goodness the reconnaissance itself was nearly completed. We were well to the south of the town now. In a few
more minutes we could turn west.

IV

How they dragged by, those minutes, interminably slow!
Tick-tick-tick—I could hear the seconds hammering by in
my head, like an uneven pulse. A flicker of sunlight spread
over our wings, gilding them, making them shine, but the
world below had darkened. It was raining in the country
through which the long train was leisurely steaming. Was it
carrying troops or freight? Any train in occupied territory
was worth while examining. I banked slightly for Dante to
see more clearly. He leaned over the side of his cockpit,
carefully counting the trucks. *Tick-tick-tick*—the engine revolutions seemed to be checking his tally. I wished he would
make haste. Apparently he found this train of great interest,
he was taking copious notes. *Tick-tick-tick*—sounded like
the scratching of his pencil—or was he tapping it against the
edge of the fuselage? Absurd thought! But there did seem
to be some unusual rattle mixed up with the more ordinary
noises of a B.E. Or were my ears playing me tricks because
of the altitude?

Dante was waving me to change course. From south to

west. It was the beginning of the journey home. And about time, too, I thought.

On completing the turn I glanced northward to get my bearings from Valenciennes. The town was much farther off than I had expected; then the wind was not due west, it was blowing us to the south. I must watch that drift on the way back; it would not do to go too far south of Arras. Forty miles to the lines, against this wind it would take us an hour at full speed losing height. I looked at my watch. We had been in the air for well over three hours. There was fuel for only one more hour with certainty. Yes, I must lose height, hurry back. *Tick-tick-tick*—something seemed to be shaking in front, near the engine. On the instrument board the revolution-counter stood fairly steady, but now I had no doubt that there was some slight, growing vibration. *Tick-tick-tick!* A menacing, horrible sound such as one might dream of in nightmare. Engine failure? The thought crossed my mind; I rejected it furiously. Those three miserable Archie shells from Denain—I had heard something strike the machine—had they done some fatal damage? Cracked a cylinder, caused an oil leak? I peered forward, afraid of my thoughts.

Dante was still busily taking notes, calmly, cold-bloodedly, unconscious of danger. He had heard nothing. Was it just my foolish imagination, after all? No, the damnable *tick-tick-tick* had become a hard knocking, louder than ever. It was sounding the knell of our hopes. . . .

Over the side I gazed downward, trying to estimate from the far distant earth the amount of our drift. It was hard to judge, the wind appeared to be north of west, but only a little. Drawing my head in, I crouched low in the cockpit to scrub with my glove at the glass top of the compass. No use; the frost was inside the glass. I could not see the compass card. A cloud passed over the sun, and at the same time the earth below began to grow dim from oncoming rain, the principal landmarks were obliterated. Dante turned to look at me anxiously, pointing ahead once or twice as if to ask the way. I shook my head in doubt. I had to guess the way home.

V

The knocking developed into a loud clanging which, I feared, was bound to terminate disastrously. It did. Suddenly. There was an explosion as loud as the bursting of a well-aimed Archie shell, pieces of metal flew past Dante's head, a big puff of blue-black smoke momentarily enveloped the engine; a flash, and the whole machine vibrated with the shock. Fire!—the thought came irresistibly into my head. Off went the switch, petrol cock closed, stick forward, throttle wide open—an engine fire might be extinguished by quick action. I dived a thousand feet off our height.

At the time my mental anguish was so great that I retain little more than a blurred impression of the whole occurrence. I had no time to think it over. After these many years, however, I feel more than ever convinced that I did the right thing, that the engine was for a few moments actually on fire quickly extinguished by the dive. We lost some valuable height, but at all events the worst catastrophe was averted, even if the inevitable end of the flight was but postponed. Slowly I flattened out, switched on again, turned the petrol cock. The engine started.

But, ye gods of machinery, how she ran! The vibration was such that the control stick jumped from my hands. This could not last, the whole machine would fall to pieces! I dared not run the engine at more than half throttle and yet I had to use it as much as possible in the hope that it would still drag us back. Where the devil were we now? Dante did not seem to know. I admired his fortitude; he sat calmly, almost rigidly in front of me, occasionally staring over the side at the gathering clouds. He must have felt horribly frightened. It is no joke to have to sit still and in silence, twelve thousand feet up in the air, behind an engine that is breaking itself into small pieces and in front of a pilot of whose thoughts you are entirely ignorant. He could not even help me steer, save by guesswork, and at that he was no better than I.

We came to a break in the clouds and, while the sun shone again for a few minutes, we looked earthwards. But it was in vain that we searched the small visible patch for familiar landmarks. Two white roads, straight as the legs of an isosceles triangle, converged; at the apex must lie a town, though we could not see it. Probably Cambrai. All right so far. A little south of our true course, but that was the fault of the north-west wind. No use heading into it more directly, it was too strong for us to fight with our failing engine-power. Better to accept the small amount of southerly drift, it might drift us over the lines. Even so we could not avoid having the main force of the wind against us.

Ahead, right across our path, rose a great mountain of cumulus. There was no going round it, we should have to fly straight through, even though the engine was running worse, the vibration tending all the time to increase, so that every now and then I had to throttle down a little more. And the compass was entirely useless; the mist had cleared to some extent from its glass, I could just make out the card, it was swinging in meaningless circles. . . .

The towering cumulus mountain stood before us like an iceberg at eight thousand feet. One last look at the ground: open rolling fields, a hedge, a track. Not a landmark. The earth faded from our sight. The machine lurched suddenly and damp, grey vapour whirled past.

VI

It was dark in the clouds and bumpy enough to make me appreciate my safety-belt. Snowflakes that smacked my face as though they had been fired from a gun rushed by, changed presently to rain-drops like whiplashes. The air became warmer; we were descending by swift stages. Every bump seemed to lower us by a hundred feet or more, and still there was nothing to steer by. I kept as straight and as even a course as my bewildered senses could suggest, but the trembling engine blurred my sight, its rattle drowned the whistling of the wind in the wires.

Where was this journey going to end? Would we cross the battle-front without knowing it, in the dark? Would the wind, less strong at lower altitudes, allow us to reach safety by a narrow margin—or were we to 'dine in Potsdam'? The suspense whilst these hopes and fears passed through my head was intolerable. Foxy was not far wrong; even at this distance of time I 'go all goosey' at the unhappy thought of it. And yet I clung to hope long enough, until in fact there was none left to cling to. I refused to believe that we might not get home, that we might fail—that we might be *captured*. I would not think of it, but even as I declared my faith in ultimate success, I found myself longing to be anywhere but in the pilot's seat of this doomed craft.

They were endless, those clouds, and the bumps they gave the machine so fierce that I had perforce to throttle the engine still more, fearful that something vital might snap under the increasing strain. Not a sight of the earth, nor of the heavens, barely enough light in the gloom to be sure of a moderately straight course. West—approximately west. In the disturbed air the speed indicator rose and fell alarmingly; it helped me to maintain an average, but that was of little use by itself. It was the wind's strength I feared, and that strength I could not measure.

Alone the altimeter held my attention. Its information was positive. Like a clock ticking away the last seconds of a condemned man's life, the needle moved ineluctably downwards, ticking off the feet: three thousand, two thousand, one thousand. Five hundred.

VII

And then, as though through a misted glass, the earth reappeared. An empty field, a deserted road with many puddles, the clustered houses of a small village, a man walking, his head bowed against the driving rain; then more fields, a clump of trees. We both stared down in dismay. There was nothing one could recognise in those few acres. I felt horribly uneasy. The sight of trenches, wire, shell-holes, the wreckage of war would have been reassuring; but this land was as peaceful as though we had left the quarrelling world behind and come from the clouds to another planet.

The ground rose sharply. A big wood lay ahead above which I should never be able to rise with the failing engine. Should I turn towards it, switch off and crash into the branches? The wreckage would be useless to the enemy, if indeed we were in their midst—and on foot we might yet escape. But there came to my mind the story of a pilot lost in the clouds as we had been and carried by a sudden change in the wind far back into friendly territory. He had jumped out of his machine and hidden in a bush—until 'captured' by the men of his own side. After all our trouble and anxiety we must not become the laughing-stock of the Flying Corps. Yet another pilot had been wafted across the Channel in a fog, and coming to ground in an unrecognised land had startled the inhabitants of Kent by asking in voluble French for the whereabouts of the Germans. . . . And also there came to my memory the landing I had made at the end of the King's patrol to ask the way, and how I had found to my joy that we were but two miles from the squadron. The same thing might happen here; a French peasant might with a word banish all our fears. I had to land, no doubt about that—the engine was finished, the ground very close—but I must land with care.

On the summit of a low hill, in a ploughed field whose soft soil in the heavy rain was fast becoming mud, I completed as good a landing as any I had ever made. The machine was safe if *we* were. Switching off I silenced the last splutters of the engine. We had been in the air over four hours.

The unusual sound of my own voice after the uproar in the machine was startling; even to me it sounded high-pitched and nervous.

'Do you think we can have crossed the lines while we were in the clouds?' I called with as much hope as I could force into my tone.

Dante climbed out of his seat, jumped down beside me.

'No,' he said, 'I'm afraid not.'

VIII

With Dante's reply I could but agree. He had merely put into words something I had not yet dared to say even to myself. His opinion that we had landed in German territory coincided with my own secret belief, and with the stating of that opinion my hopes were virtually extinguished. A last spark remained among the embers: I asked him to go back on foot in the direction whence we had flown, as far as the brow of the hill. From behind a hedge he would be able to see the village, spy out the land, watch who came. If French peasants all was well; if no one, we would have time to deliberate; if the enemy. . . . He nodded assent and jogged off in his heavy flying-kit through the squelching mud. In days gone by he had done good work as an aerial gunner, as observer he had been painstaking, indefatigable; in several combats he had acted as calmly as during the recent trying moments of our descent. Now he made his last reconnaissance whilst I stood by the machine preparing for my own final duty.

Not twenty seconds passed before I heard his shout. The words shocked, yet did not surprise me; they but brought to a climax a morning of anguish such as one is not often asked to endure.

'Look out,' he cried. 'Germans! Hundreds of them—they're coming! Quick—can you light her up?'

Yes, I could do that. I had never thought of it before, and there was not much time left now. But I knew that I could do it.

In a cubby-hole behind the pilot's seat was stored a flare. I had seen it there many a time; but to this day I do not know whether it was intended solely for setting machines on fire or whether it had originally been meant to serve as a signal of distress for machines coming down in the Channel. Perhaps both emergencies had been envisaged. At all events it served my purpose well enough, although in this as in so many other matters no instructions had ever been given. But I knew my way about that aeroplane, and I knew the easiest of the petrol connections to get at. My one fear was that after our long flight there would not be enough petrol left for a big flare-up.

For the last of my anxieties, however, there was fortunately no ground. A good three or four gallons of petrol remained, and as I wrenched away the rubber connection a steady, clear stream gushed forth. I struck the flare. Thrust it forward. And the sudden blast of the flames as they shot up and spread was like a gasp of astonishment sent up to the weeping skies. I sprang back, my face scorched by the blaze.

For an instant we both stood watching, gaining some small satisfaction from the success of our final endeavour; then

Dante ran forward to throw maps and reconnaissance notes into the flames. Nothing should be left for the enemy, nothing save only our wretched selves. That we could not remedy; we were burdened by flying-kit, mud held back our heavy boots; the Germans were coming up on two sides, at a run. We pushed more things into the fire, making sure that all were destroyed. On the rear mounting the Lewis gun pointed defiantly at the heavens. The flames licked about it, rising from the fiercely burning fire, roaring in that same west wind which had completed our downfall.

I thought of Shoreham. I had seen many crashes since then, but no fire. It had been my first experience in the Flying Corps and now—for a time—it must be my last. But at least there was no tortured victim in the crumbling front seat. No human being had suffered from my piloting, except a few of the enemy. And yet both machines—here as at Shoreham—were B.E.2c.s. There must be some significance in the flames, something of my own self ascending in smoke and fire from the aeroplane in which I had dreamed and hoped, fought, striven and feared. . . .

'You speak German, don't you?' Dante said. 'Better say something to them.'

I turned away from the machine. Large numbers of German soldiers were beginning to appear from over the brow of the hill. They were out of breath from hard running and as they came near they slowed down to a walk. Through the centre of their long, ragged line a man on horseback approached at a gallop, drew rein within ten yards of us. He wore a spiked helmet, a sheathed sword hung by his side and upon the shoulders of his long coat were the insignia of some rank or other. I judged him to be a senior N.C.O., but it seemed wise to give him the benefit of the doubt.

'*Herr Leutnant,*' I called, 'we are English officers. We have had trouble with our engine and have been forced to come down. We wish to surrender.'

Something had to be said by way of introduction, but I felt rather an ass making such an obvious speech. Especially as I had not used so much German since before the war; I fancy my words must have smacked too much of the courtly surrenders of another age, they did not fit in with the angry rudeness so necessary to twentieth-century warfare. They certainly puzzled the man on the horse. '*Ja*,' was all that he could find to say.

And then the Lewis gun spoke its last words to the enemy, barking like a watchdog at the approach of danger. The ammunition had become red-hot; it burst with a series of loud crackling explosions. At that the horse took charge of the man; together they galloped off the field.

IX

The men who presently advanced towards us were from a German air-squadron stationed less than a mile away. In a short time we were surrounded by a dozen or more young flying-officers.

I have today no warmer a feeling of friendship, no deeper an understanding of the men of the German Flying Corps than I had on the day of my capture. And this for the very good reason that in the course of one winter's afternoon in 1915 I learnt so to appreciate their qualities that no mode or trend of opinion can ever change my sentiments. They did much more than spare our lives; they spared our pride. With fellow-feeling for airmen in distress they solaced our despair. Towards us, captives from an alien and hated race, they made no gesture of anger or of reproach. Their hands were raised; but to salute us. They spoke to us not with words of triumph, of wrath or of scorn, but with a ready sympathy for our plight, a knowledge of all that our misfortune must mean to us. We were their enemies, British, and at their mercy; but they did not show by word or deed that they were aware of the fact. It may have been wholly that much-exaggerated 'comradeship of the air' which linked us, but I prefer to believe that our mutual understanding ran deeper. We wore the uniforms of our respective countries, we stood for different causes, but, beneath all the superficialities, we knew that we were actuated by the same motives. Youth, adventure, high spirits—those things wound up for us the mainspring of life. We would have fought just as well without propaganda; we had no need for bitter hatred. So may it have been in the days of chivalry.

After the first stiffness and formality were over, one of

them asked me: 'But why were you flying on this of all days—in weather too bad for any of us to go up?'

'Just paying a little round of visits to certain places such as Valenciennes,' I answered, anxious not to give anything away.

'Valenciennes?' he exclaimed. He seemed amazed. 'But have you been there often?'

'Once too often!' I replied ruefully. Whereat he and the others were good enough to laugh.

'And what made you come down?' they wanted to know.

For answer I led the way to the front of the machine and pointed at the broken cylinder. I was never able to find out what had been the first cause of the trouble, although at the time I naturally suspected faulty lubrication. It may have been Archie, but I doubt it. A flaw in the metal, a worn bearing—without taking the engine down there was no possibility of making sure. And, after all, engine failure was not uncommon; only unpleasant. But it was plain enough to even the most unaccustomed eye that no machine could hold the air long with one out of eight cylinders almost entirely absent. The German officers clicked their tongues and shook their heads at the evil sight. They smiled at us understandingly and murmured their sympathy in a way that implied a share in our sorrow, a compassion for such ill-luck.

I am not sure it was through no fault of theirs that later on, while we were in the mess, certain men of the squadron went through the pockets of the coats we had left hanging outside. It was not an 'official' purloining that deprived us of money and cigarettes.

Long afterwards I found that our point of landing was within six miles of the front lines. Five more minutes' flying time would have seen us safely over.

X

It was a phrase used during luncheon—at which we were the honoured guests—that brought home to me the full meaning of our calamity. We had been talking shop with so much animation that I had nearly forgotten the circumstances of capture and the misery of being a prisoner of war, when one of the pilots happened to ask me if I enjoyed reading German books. Reading, he remarked, would lighten '*die furchtbare Langeweile*'. And all at once I perceived that in those words the future was summed up for me: the frightful boredom—of being held captive, of sitting idly waiting for the time to pass, for the war to be over; while all the time these men would be able to go on flying, fighting, achieving something however small, at any rate living, adventuring. The sudden realisation of coming inaction was less merciful than a blow on the head, it was sentence of living death; and it was on the tip of my tongue to retort that I had no intention of sitting still to endure it, that there was such a thing as escape and that I should take the first opportunity to try it. But where they had been courteous, I must be tactful. Already I was learning that of a prisoner's valour by far the better part is dissimulation.

But that night, after we had been transferred to less hospitable surroundings in the town of St Quentin, the thought returned to me with renewed vigour. I could never resign myself to spending the remainder of the war in prison; the hope of flying again—all that was left to me—*that* I refused to surrender. It simply could not be that I had flown for the last time. I must get away from this intolerable captivity; I must get back to the squadron, to the barge on the River Lys, to the tall line of poplars and to the slippery mud of that narrow L-shaped aerodrome. I saw now how much all those things had meant to me. . . . Boredom? Yes, I had been bored there sometimes, but not as I was going to be bored if I did not at once strive for freedom. Life in the barge was dull no doubt, yet outside it there had been action, flying, fights in the air, work to do; prospects, distant perhaps, of something startling happening to the war. It was hard to lose so much, impossible not to wish to regain everything by a bold yet cunning stroke.

If only I could get away from my captors—sometime, somehow—elude them, run, hide, cross the frontiers of Belgium and Holland; or else sneak cautiously through the trenches on some dark night. I didn't care how it was done so long as I could return to the squadron I had left that morning. It would not be easy, on the face of it I could see that much; I must think it out calmly, with determination. And then some day I should see again the Lys curved like a scimitar, the poplars straight as well-drilled soldiers, the grey barge—with men waiting open-mouthed in the mess, to whom I would tell my story, to whom I would explain the events of this day, explain why I had been forced to land. And the major would smile rather more broadly than usual and put just a little warmth into his 'Well done!' And Growl would clap me on the back and say, 'By jove, young fellow-me-lad, come and have a drink! . . .'

Victory when at length it came was not like that. It never is. Success, hard won, can never be as sweet as the sanguine dreams of youth would make it. For it is in the nature of things that every real achievement must come a little too late. When next I flew over Merville, the quiet fields near the river were pitted with shell-holes, the stems of the poplars were broken and the barge had gone from the Lys.

The friendly reception of the German flying-officers had ill-prepared me for the night spent in a cell in St Quentin gaol. Lonely, dejected, I was overwhelmed by the day's disaster. Memories of the past months came to taunt me. Foxy's titter: so this was 'Potsdam', this moist foul-smelling cell? Rare Earths would have been able to collect some fine samples from the walls, let alone the floors. Where was Wilhelm in all this? At the German squadron they had not been able to tell me anything about him. At any rate he must be in hospital, better than being here unwounded. 'What would you do if your engine were to fail over Valenciennes?' That damned question! And how had I answered it? I supposed that I ought to have landed unseen in a forest somewhere to the east, waited till dark, made a bolt for the frontier and freedom. . . . And my leave had been due at Christmas!

Outside, somewhere in the town, a clock boomed the hours. The long vibrating strokes rang in my ears, echoed in my heart: '*Escape-Escape-Escape!*' I prayed that when Opportunity came my way she would not be 'veiled like an Eastern bride', and that I should be prompt to recognise her.

But I am glad that I did not know how long it would take.

Part Two

4

The Wings Grow Again

I

His Majesty* lit a cigarette, inhaled, blew out the match.
'And what are you going to do now?' he asked.
He had moved to one side whilst lighting that cigarette,
so that my eyes were no longer upon his face. I looked out
of an open window upon the Green Park. The trees were in
leaf, the sun shone. A faint breeze ruffled the loose-hanging
curtains and bore in from Piccadilly and Hyde Park Corner
the subdued roar of London, a roar that to my unaccustomed
ears was like a distant roll of drums, an eternal call to arms.
It was May, 1918.
'What are you going to do now?'
The King had come forward again, between me and the
light, and now his head was framed by the tall window and
the green grass beyond. London was behind him. The call
to arms came from over his shoulder.
'I'm going back to France, sir.'
I had no hesitation; France it must be. I had given the
matter a great deal of thought, and my answer to that particular question was decided upon long before I reached
Buckingham Palace. But I have no doubt that, had I been
in any uncertainty, those twenty minutes of the King's audience would have compelled me to make up my mind without
possibility of change. For the telling of my story had re-
awakened old voices heard upon the banks of the Lys, in the
keen air above Artois, and in the less wholesome air of St
Quentin gaol. And, as I see it, the reasons for such a re-
awakening are easy to understand, since after long years
* King George V.

of endeavour, of frequent failure and occasional despair, the great, the longed-for, the romantic climax had come. Fortune had smiled—if rather late in the day—and the adventure seemed to be concluded.

Seemed—for I saw clearly that it was not yet ended. Real success could only be claimed when I had completed the circle, returned to the point from which I had started. . . .

'I'm going back to France!'

I had caught myself wondering, before the interview, how the King would receive this declaration of mine. Would he, like certain kindly people at the Air Ministry and elsewhere, say: 'No, no, my boy, you've done enough'? I hoped not. The remark made me shudder, for they were dead who had 'done enough'.

The question that came by way of reply was more to the point. It showed understanding, not only of the attitude of those in authority, but also, I think, of my personal desires and their probable frustration. Just four words:

'Will they let you?'

I said rather meekly: 'I think so, sir.'

It was not quite true. I was beginning to be afraid 'they' would *not* let me go. The fear had become more real during the past week or two, but I think it had been growing ever since the day when the train carried me from St Quentin to the Rhine.

II

That was an afternoon of unalleviated melancholy, of sadness growing more intense at each rhythmical click of the wheels upon the rails. For as long as we were in France some faint hope still beat within me that something would happen—that the train might be derailed, that a bomb might fall from the empty sky to kill my captors, even that a sudden and wholly unexpected offensive by the Allies might sweep through the trench lines into the back areas, so that presently I should see cavalry or armoured cars dash across the rolling countryside to stop the train. Hope clung to me through Bohain and Busigny on to Le Cateau—had not British troops fought there? There might yet be survivors, stragglers cut off from the retreat, hidden among the friendly woods and villages of this last corner of France. . . . The express train rushed on. The sort of 'something' which I so wanted to happen did not occur. It seldom does.

At dusk we crossed the Belgian frontier.

'Do we pass through Mons?' I asked.

'Mons?'

'Yes, where a battle was fought in the early days—the first battle in which the English were engaged?'

'Never heard of it,' was the answer. And at that the war, active operations at all events, became suddenly immeasurably distant. . . .

Between Liège and the German frontier the train chanced to run at reduced speed. A dark night; from the compartment windows I could see nothing of the countryside; but, aware that only a few miles to the north lay Holland and freedom, a wild hope seized me. I tried the lavatory. The German guard who escorted me kept his foot in the door, the window was fixed shut, and it was plain that there would be no time to break through it before the guard took action. Nothing doing. A few minutes later the train ran into Herbesthal, first station inside Germany. It was a long time before I came so near to the Dutch frontier again.

A change of trains and of guards at Cologne, a long wait and a longer journey up the Rhine valley; at four in the morning, leaving the train at Mainz, we marched uphill into the Citadel barracks. There, in the company of some four hundred other prisoners—Russian, French, British and Belgian—I settled in to spend my first Christmas in captivity and, presently, to make my first feeble scratchings in a tunnel.

A futile affair, the Germans must have thought it; for of course they knew. The entrance was in the basement next to the bath-house and the fact that we, the diggers, made use of the bath-house every afternoon yet came out of it dirtier than when we went in was rather too obvious to be tolerated. In January (1916) half a dozen of us were transferred at a moment's notice to Weilburg, a pleasant little place—or so it would have seemed to eyes less jaundiced than those of war-prisoners—where we were lodged in a large two-storey house, formerly a school for N.C.O.'s in the picturesque valley of the Lahn.

Down the steep and wooded sides of that encompassing valley, by some freak effect of acoustics there rolled before the end of winter a distant thunder of gunfire. Barely audible yet unmistakable, from a hundred and fifty miles away: the remote thunder of massed artillery at Verdun. An inspiring sound, that raised our eyes to the echoing clouds and sent us, paradoxically, underground, to tunnel hopefully from a disused cellar. Russian officers had already started the dig before our coming; we joined them enthusiastically in an atmosphere of night-time conspiracy, driving the shaft forward with a will, thrusting it out beneath the camp boundary; only to fail within a few yards of success. Driven too near the surface, the roof began to cave beneath the unexpected weight of an exceptional snowfall; shored up, it withstood the pressure until the first thaw; then gave way to the heavy stamp of German guards marching overhead.

A fragment of wood from a crate, used in shoring up the roof, bore the barely decipherable name of one of our own accomplices. Whereat the German commandant summoned the dozen or so British prisoners before him and, pink-faced with agitation, denounced our crime: this was a *Schweinerei!* It was forbidden to escape! If we made any further attempt we would be immediately shot dead: *sofort todtgeschossen!* . . . Without delay we started to evolve new plans, learning the tricks of the trade as we went: the making of false keys to open the doors of German offices, the typing —on a 'borrowed' typewriter—of forged passes to facilitate travel by rail, the copying of such rare fragments of maps as the French were able to purchase from sympathetic Alsatians among the guards. In the end we were not too badly equipped; but in the execution of our plans nothing went right for us. A new tunnel ran into solid rock; a well-planned exit in laundry baskets was foiled by a last-minute change in camp routine that put the baskets out of our reach. One night in April, helping to fuse the camp lights to aid an escape attempt, I was caught in the act. Enjoyed the experience of a court martial in Frankfurt, less the ensuing month of solitary confinement in the Weilburg prison; so that it came as a relief to be transferred, at the end of May, to a new and supposedly superior establishment at Friedberg-in-Hessen.

But however clean and well regulated as a prisoner-of-war camp, from an escaper's point of view it was an unpromising place. Its two modern barrack buildings, surrounded by a palisade and two rows of sentry-guarded wire, stood in flat, open country that discouraged all thought of a direct attempt upon the defences. A tunnel? Impossible indoors; the barrack basements, daily inspected by the enemy, had cement floors above concrete foundations. We began to dig in the open; sinking a shaft in the half-acre of wasteland allotted to prisoners for the planting of small 'gardens'; concealing its mouth ingeniously enough within a summer-house tent, distributing the spoil evenly over our patch of land embellished with potted plants, obtained through the camp's canteen. Throughout the summer we worked at it, carved our way through firm clay soil, hid the entrance beneath some three feet of earth at the end of each day's stint, effaced all trace of work upon the tent's floor with a liberal sprinkling of granite chips. By mid-August, with more than thirty yards dug, we had passed, according to our careful measurements, beneath the wire and the palisade, beyond the outer line of sentries, to reach a fold in the land bordering an orchard. The time had come to break surface.

At that same moment luck deserted us. An unrelated escape attempt from the nearby *Kommandantur* roused to violent activity the hitherto unsuspecting Germans; a camp-wide search was followed by a general digging up of the 'gardens' that revealed, in the end, our tunnel's entrance. . . . The Germans were even more surprised than angry. 'Why,' one of them remonstrated with me, 'why do you want to escape? It's not unpleasant here, and even if you succeeded in getting out you'd never get across the frontier.' I was to hear it many times again later on: '*Ueber die Grenze kommen Sie nie.*' It was, just then, the least of our worries.

Other plans were considered, some wild, some desperate. Late in September we tried one of the most fanciful. As many a would-be escaper had noticed there was a close similarity, in texture as in colour, between the overcoats worn by German and Russian officers. By friendly exchange and barter two Russian coats had been obtained and, the cut being different, suitable alterations made by the camp tailor, a gallant Frenchman who cheerfully risked imprison-

ment to score off the *sales Boches*. Accessories, caps, bits and
pieces of equipment were collected from two other prisoners
who had long considered the scheme and worked upon it
but no longer believed it to be feasible. At length ready, the
camp routine meticulously observed, we put it to the test.
At nine o'clock on a morning of hazy sunshine, three of us—
two as German officers, the third a sort of secretary-assistant
in civilian clothes—marched out of the *Kommandantur* to
which we had gone one by one, ostensibly to collect food-
parcels, in reality to make a quick change from khaki to field-
grey in a cubby hole beneath the stairs. Marched some thirty
yards towards the gate most generally used by the authorities; taking pains to advance only at a slow and dignified
pace whilst I, the one German-speaker, almost paralysed
with stage-fright, talked incessantly to cover the silence of
the other two and anxiously watched the behaviour of the
sentries. Within ten yards of the gate I dared to raise my
voice; barked out the magic word: '*Aufmachen!*' It did the
trick. The sentries sprang to attention, clicked heels; one
of them rattled keys, turned the lock, flung open the gate,
stood back. And then, as for the immortal *Mr Toad*, the
soldiers all saluted as we marched along the road. . . .

Marched on in agony of discomfort both mental and physi-
cal; across country, over open fields, past staring peasants;
marched half-strangled by the closely packed provisions
tightly strapped beneath our German overcoats. Marched
for two hours towards the wooded slopes of the Taunus;
reached them at last, climbed high up the hillside and,
discarding our German uniforms to reappear as nonde-
script civilians, rested in security waiting for nightfall. . . . A
still day of late summer whose deep silence was broken
intermittently by that immensely distant yet immediately
recognisable rumbling: the thunder of guns massed upon
the Western Front. 'March to the sound of the guns'—no,
we couldn't do that. Coming down from the hillside at dusk,
we marched east. Passed to the north of Homburg and then,
on successive nights, to the north of Frankfurt, to the east
of Hanau, south to Aschaffenburg, narrowly avoiding
unexpected perils on the long road to Switzerland. Before
dawn on the fifth day an error in navigation led us to camp
at the foot of a low embankment; revealed for what it was

when, at first light, a train rolled surprisingly overhead. The sharp-eyed driver spotted us, raised the alarm at the next station; the railway staff came out in force, surrounded us in the woods, marched us of to gaol.

A month's solitary confinement in the town prison at Friedberg; then, for me, a journey via Berlin to Fort Zorndorf, a few miles to the north-east of Cüstrin and notorious as a special camp for persistent escapers. No one could break out of it, they said. No one. On a bleak January afternoon, unkindly tricking the commandant who had invited us to his house amid the trees outside the fort to discuss camp routine, three of us eluded our escorts and, vaulting a fence, made a bolt for it and got away. Almost at once the alerted guards were in hot pursuit; we had to sprint through the woods at top speed for the better part of a mile and we were none too fit. One lagged behind, was overtaken by the guards and hauled back to the fort. The surviving pair of us kept on, shedding khaki overcoats as we went, heading north into the darkening pine-forest.

Our aim was to outwit the enemy by reaching, at dawn, a branch-line railway station beyond any point he could reasonably expect us to make. A night of considerable discomfort followed, memorable chiefly for the distance covered: forty-five miles across country in under fifteen hours, for the most part against driving rain turning to sleet. Thinly clad in makeshift civilian clothes, with scarcely any food, it was far from pleasant. But we made the objective in good time; took train for Berlin and, absorbed into the crowd of fourth-class passengers, thought ourselves safe. Two stations later a guard, sent specially from the fort to head us off, came on board and held us up at pistol-point. The third man of our team had been unable, on recapture, to destroy his map; it had given away our intended route. . . .

Ten days in Cüstrin gaol. Back to the fort. Out again for a night attempt in February. This time to exploit a scheme patiently evolved by some French officers who, prematurely transferred to another camp, had bequeathed it to three of us, together with all its equipment. Deep snow lay on the ramparts when, on the appointed night, we sallied from a casemate on top of the fort and concealed by white overalls, crawled unseen past a line of patrolling sentries, bearing with us as well as our kit the three parts of a ladder to be assembled in the ditch for the scaling of the fort's outer wall, an obstacle rising up a sheer thirty feet to the level of the surrounding country. The ladder, brilliantly contrived by the French out of chair legs reinforced with angle-irons taken from camp bedsteads, was just over twenty-nine feet long. Enough; but no allowance had been made for the unforeseen foot of packed ice and snow now overhanging the wall's crown. With the ladder in position before dawn, when the night guard in the ditch had been withdrawn and the daytime guard on the fort's summit had not yet come on—an observed interval of ten minutes—we found to our dismay that we were unable to surmount the slippery ice-cap. No remedy was available in the time; we had no pick and fingers alone could not break the ice, nor could the ladder support more than one man at a time. . . . When the German garrison gathered in the ditch for the morning parade they stared in consternation, barked their displeasure, and took us back into the fort.

Three months solitary in Cüstrin gaol on a charge of stealing angle-irons from the Kaiser's bedsteads, then back to the fort to plan anew. To scheme, to discuss, to argue, sometimes to quarrel, but always with the one end in view: to get out of Germany and back into the war. Of course we knew well enough that not one man in a hundred of us would ever succeed—and, knowing it, some gave up, settled down to learn Russian. They were wise. But the obstinate few whose youthful unwisdom transcended the mere need for adventure to alleviate the tedium of captivity clung with an almost religious fervour to the belief that Chance would some day reward their restless perseverance. '*Ueber die Grenze kommen Sie nie*'—we knew *that* was nonsense; others had crossed over before us. Nor did we forget that the German stood in Belgium where he had no right to be; he must be thrown out before the war could end; and in that ousting we intended to play our part. But for me as, I suppose, for any young pilot there was something more: the unflagging desire to fly again, to climb above the clouds, to hear anew the steady hum of a smooth-running engine and the comforting music of the wind in the wires.

With the German authorities now striving to efface the

'. . . at least a wing-commander'. Return from ground-attack, 28 September, 1918
Sketch by the author

Johnny: Captain John Speaks DFC, RFC and RAF (American)

Bloody Bob: Lieutenant Robert A. Caldwell DFC, RFC and
RAF (Canadian)

sinister reputation of Fort Zorndorf as a 'special' camp, new
British prisoners were brought in, some straight from capture.
From one of them, a Scot and a pilot, I learned of great
changes in aviation, of new machines and new methods, of
whole squadrons of single-seat fighters flying in formation,
engaged in daily combat. Heard too of those achieving fame
in the crowded skies of north-eastern France. The Germans
sang loud the praises of Immelmann and Boelcke; the
French glorified Guynemer. The British, for sound reasons,
did not advertise their successful pilots; but from my Scottish
friend I learned of many names new to me. One in particular,
that of Captain Albert Ball, stuck fast in my memory. . . .

In August (1917) a few of us were unexpectedly transferred
to the camp of Ströhen Moor in Hanover. An unhealthy
spot and ill-equipped, with dysentery afflicting its three or four
hundred all-British inmates; worse than that, already before
our arrival there had been so many escape attempts that,
with the Germans thoroughly alerted, there were few sound
opportunities left. Eventually, after a succession of minor
failures, six of us evolved a bold scheme in which, once
again, I was to wear German uniform. This time, dis-
guised as a *Landsturm* guard—complete with home-made
gear and dummy rifle—I was to lead out of one of the side-
gates the other five dressed as British orderlies and wheeling
a baggage cart 'to the railway station', a more or less daily
occurrence. Weeks were spent building up the rifle, contrived with odds and ends of iron and wood, with a bolt
mechanism made from pieces of tin-can shaped and sand-
papered to look like steel. At long last ready, we paraded early
one morning. Barking out German commands at my appar-
rently reluctant and appropriately slouching crew, I led the
way to the gate; and showing a forged pass, demanded its
opening.

A scheme of such effrontery deserved to succeed. And
succeed it did: until, outside the camp, a sharp-eyed sentry—
who from long service at Ströhen knew many of the prisoners
by sight—chanced to recognise as officers first one then
another of the 'orderlies'. I suppose we were lucky not to be
'*todtgeschossen*'. . . . Gaol was followed by a court martial
at Hanover—I forget on what charges—and a three-month
sentence, served partly at Ströhen, partly at Neunkirchen

F

to which about eighty of us were moved in November.

Neunkirchen was one of several camps the Germans established in the Saar in the hope that the presence of officer prisoners of war would ward off allied bombing of the area. The hope proved vain; to the remote thunder of guns on the West Front there was added presently the sharper thudding of local anti-aircraft guns, to us a welcome sound. But the very nature of the camp—a single building in the centre of the town, its small courtyard overlooked by neighbouring houses and heavily guarded—made escape more than usually difficult. A tunnel was the best bet; and throughout long snowy weeks of winter we worked at it. Organised and equipped, it expertly made ready to evacuate a good half of the camp's inmates, providing many with sketch-maps and home-made compasses; thrust out, once again, to within feet of the proposed exit. And then the snows melted and the rains came, and the camp's drainage system was choked. Drainage engineers, brought in to inspect and repair the damage, laid bare the tunnel's well-concealed entrance.

A fortnight in the local gaol brought my total time in solitary confinement to eight months, with success as far away as ever. But with the spring came new hope. Neunkirchen camp was to be closed, the prisoners transferred to camps deeper in Germany; at the same time an Anglo-German exchange scheme came into operation whereby long-term prisoners were released to enjoy the relative freedom of internment in Holland. Still believing in ultimate success, I refused the exchange; but the authorities insisted: I must go to the transit-camp to certify my refusal lest Germany be accused of holding prisoners back. In mid-April half a dozen of us were moved to Aachen. Close enough to the Dutch frontier certainly, but, we learned, for a stay of no more than thirty-six hours.

A daunting prospect. A challenge to all the knowledge and experience gained from the years of effort. A new camp, only the daylight hours in which to survey its defences, to note its routine, to devise a plan. Only one evening in which to make good an escape, one night in which to march a roundabout twenty miles so as to reach the frontier—and cross it!—before daybreak. The escape must go unnoticed by the camp guards, since with the frontier so close it would be easy to alert the area once the alarm had been raised. For much the same reason it would be impossible to lie up near the frontier, study the landscape and cross over on a second night: as soon as we were missed from the camp during the day the border guards would be reinforced. Nor was the country easy to cross; hilly, wooded, intersected by small streams, in the open it was studded as well by farm buildings as by mining villages. Quite a problem! But this time the luck was on our side. My chosen companion—Beverley Robinson, a Canadian pilot who had served his time at Zorndorf—was a tower of strength, moreover he possessed an excellent map. By a narrow margin we made it. . . . Nearly two and a half years had gone by since a train's lavatory window had barred my way to this same frontier. Now, humbling circumstance, it was through a lavatory ventilator that we climbed from our camp into a lavatory of the adjoining German transit camp; thence down an open drain, under the wire, away into the night, unseen.

It was still night when we reached the frontier. Before dawn we crossed it unawares; strode on anxiously, checking our position by map and compass at first light. Verified it again from the cover of a bramble patch as day broadened, until no possible doubt remained. '*Ueber die Grenze kommen Sie nie*'? Rubbish! We stood in Holland. Success had come at last. Sweet success!

III

I cannot for a moment pretend that these memories of escape 'flashed' through my head while I answered the King's questions. But all of them and many more were lodged in that mysterious locality known as the back of one's mind. And in the effort to extract events necessary to make a brief and coherent story, I found that the whole lot had come floating to the surface.

With the result that when, at the end of the interview, I left the Palace it was to seek forthwith that sanction which alone could crown the long adventure. A taxi took me to the newly created Air Ministry, then in the Strand at the Hotel Cecil. There from a senior but sympathetic friend I begged a straight answer to the essential question: Would 'they' let me return to the front in France?

To my relief I heard him say that he thought it could be arranged. The trouble was that hitherto no one captured flying in France had been allowed to return to fly in France, because—and I had to admit the truth of this—capture was one of the things most likely to happen to an air-pilot. And apart from the vague possibility of an officer, captured for the second time, being an enemy agent, there was the more serious probability of his being harshly treated by the Germans. Personally I thought that the likelihood of being recognised on capture would be exceedingly remote, and afterwards—but, touching wood, I had no intention of being captured.

'It may happen, however,' my friend insisted, 'and therefore it will be best if you adopt another name when you get to the front.'

'When I get to the front! But how *am* I to get there?'

'Well—I think if you go back to your training squadron, pass through and *say nothing*, the Air Ministry will forget about you in time. Then, when a batch of pilots is sent out to France, your name won't be noticed amongst the others. And I promise you my department will make no objections.'

I took him at his word and returned to London Colney where I had been posted shortly after landing in England. I had taken no leave, for I knew that I could always get occasional days and week-ends off while learning to fly. There was plenty of time. The great German attack was held up; there would be a return push in the summer, driving on through the winter; and the next spring, with the Americans properly in the field at last, the final battles would be fought. I curbed my impatience and took up the 'new' flying with enthusiasm.

It was a long job. Longer than I had expected. Slowly I passed through the usual business of engine-fitting, rigging, machine-gunnery, and graduation from the Avro to the Sopwith Pup, to the Spad, finally to the S.E.5a. I was shown all the mysteries of aerobatics and taught—very badly—how to fly in formation. At length, in August, I was ready. The Air Ministry said nothing: 'they' seemed indeed to have forgotten all about me. Young pilots who had started their training just before me began to move off overseas. Only the shortage of S.E.5 practice machines held me up until the middle of the month.

And then one morning orders came for me to join a School of Aerial Fighting in Yorkshire.

IV

There was something very puzzling about this posting to Yorkshire. It was not absolutely essential for a pilot, especially for one who had been to France before, to pass through an Aerial Fighting School; to my own knowledge several fledgelings had gone direct from the training squadron to France. I had now all the necessary qualifications and my friend at the Air Ministry had kept his word about letting my name through in the ordinary way, without mention of capture or escape. Why, therefore, had I of all others been selected to go so far north as Yorkshire? A Fighting School was, of course, another step on the way to the front, but it was also another delay. I began to see in this move the action of some well-meaning but misguided individual, someone who saw that by sending me to Yorkshire a little more time would be gained, another chance that I might change my mind. After the course of fighting instruction there were other stations to which 'they' might send me; Home Defence loomed menacingly near.

With these uneasy suspicions in mind I kept my eyes open as soon as I stepped into the headquarters office of the Fighting School. Presently my name amongst others was called out by one of the staff, and on hearing it a clerk rose from a corner of the room, crossed over and handed me a small bundle of papers.

I glanced through them. There were a couple of letters forwarded to me by the Air Ministry, a claim for some allowance or other, and an open envelope with my name in one corner and the commanding-officer's in the other. An envelope which at once increased my suspicions and my fears of interference. I turned it over in my hands: what was it?—a sort of letter of introduction? In that case the open flap and my name in the corner gave me a right to

read it. . . . Dodging behind the line of waiting pilots, I
opened it and read.

When I came to the end I fancy I must have smiled at
the luck which had allowed this letter to fall into my hands
before it reached the C.O. It was from a fairly high-placed
and influential friend at the Air Ministry. It contained a
flattering account of my captivity and escape; but it ended
with the statement that, whereas I was anxious to proceed
overseas, it was considered undesirable that I should return
to France. Italy was suggested. . . .

In the days of my captivity I had learnt that on recapture,
after an attempted escape, the first thing to do was to destroy
efficiently the maps and other incriminating documents one
was carrying. Months of concentration upon the one subject
of escape had brought such lessons in habit up to the level
of instinct. In this office of the school on the distant Yorkshire
coast, seeing that I was in danger of recapture, the instinct
asserted itself. I tore the envelope and the letter to small
pieces. And no one in that gathering of newly fledged pilots
realised that I was escaping again.

Two days later, the school being greatly overcrowded, it
was decided to send away a batch of those pilots who had
some previous tuition in aerial fighting and sufficient flying-
hours to their credit. The majority of these pilots were young
Canadians and Americans serving in the British forces, lighthearted, keen for adventure in the air, elated that their stay
in Yorkshire had been cut short. They left the school singing
and cheering happily, for their orders were to report at the
Air Ministry on their way to France. And I can testify that
they sang and cheered and were happy, because it happened
that I was one of them.

V

I had no idea of the intricate organisation which had
grown up for the disposal of pilots in France. I had imagined
that, as on a previous occasion, I would have to wander
about looking for a headquarters or an office of sorts, that
I might have difficulty in finding anyone who cared a damn
where I went to or when, but that by the end of twenty-four

hours I should somehow have drifted off to a squadron and that there the fun would begin at once.

It wasn't at all like that. The number of officials at Boulogne surprised me; it seemed dismally certain that the army in France had been overtaken by efficiency. They were like ushers in a cinema, inspecting your tickets before letting you through to the performance. And as in a theatre, so here there were clear distinctions between tickets of different value. Staff ticket-holders were bowed into cars and driven to the stalls and boxes; subalterns and other ranks crammed into the same old tumbledown trains which would eventually deposit them within walking distance of the pit. As for air-pilots, we were the cheap seats. But instead of allowing us to go straight up to the gallery, they pushed us into a train that steamed off in the wrong direction—away from the front!

It was not until we had passed Etaples and were almost at Berck that I understood we were going to a sort of live-stock depot known as a 'Pilots' Pool'. We arrived late at night and I could neither see nor discover anything of the place until the following morning. Then to my horror I found that I was back in prison. . . . The offices were set apart and labelled 'No Admittance' and 'Keep Out'. Here and there guards were mounted on sentry-go. Why, there was even a stretch of barbed-wire about the place and over the sand dunes!

And the reports which other pilots gave me were not encouraging. The place was full to overflowing, there had not been many demands from squadrons recently, there was a waiting list a mile long. Many of the pilots did not care; they had been out to France several times before and were content to wait their turn. Some of them had been waiting two or three weeks, and were expecting to stay for as many more. . . . 'They also serve who only stand and wait . . .' I was bored and discouraged.

During my first day more than twenty pilots arrived; not half a dozen left. There was nothing to do all day and nothing but a bar to sit in at night. On the second day the same thing happened: many officers coming in, few going out. Someone who had been to the office told me that the list of pilots was in a terrible muddle; the single-seater people were mixed up with the heavy bombers, and it might be weeks before things

were straightened out. There was no flying, and on the coast
we could not hear the guns. The wind hummed, but in wires
that were barbed, not streamlined.

Early on the morning of the third day I went to the office
to have a look round. There were many pilots hanging about,
some old, some new; they were giving particulars about
themselves to be entered on the new lists which were being
compiled by a couple of clerks. Some of us strolled into the
orderly-room—the C.O. being absent at breakfast—to look
at the lists, at the numbers of those units requiring pilots,
and so on. I was reading through some routine orders when
all at once I caught sight of the new list of single-seater
pilots. It was lying beside the typewriter upon which it had
just been made out by one of the clerks, ready for submitting
to the C.O. as soon as he came in.

I glanced down the list. It was very long, covering two
pages of foolscap gummed together. Pilot's names were thick
on the paper as autumn leaves. It took me some time to reach
my own—near the foot of the page! Just as I found it one of
the clerks came by.

'I say, Corporal, surely my name ought to be higher than
that,' I exclaimed, bitter with disappointment. 'I've been here
three days already. I can't wait for ever!'

He laughed as he came up to me. He was a friendly
sort of fellow.

'Some of them have been here for three weeks, sir. But
perhaps there's been a mistake. Let me see—which is your
name?'

I reached forward to point it out. As I did so my sleeve
caught against some light object upon the table.

'Look out!' cried the Corporal.

But he was just too late. A river of ink streamed over the
page and cascaded to the floor. The bottle rolled slowly
through the black stream, splashing over the names.

'O-o-h . . .' said the corporal. 'You . . .' He paused, only
the regulation respect for rank preventing a comment upon
my parentage. 'You—you've spilt the ink!'

'Couldn't help it,' I told him. 'Bottle on table—uncorked
—caught in my sleeve—an accident. I can't tell you how
sorry I am!'

He was kind enough to be pacified at once.

'That's all right, sir; can't be helped. Trouble is it's the only completed list we've got. And the C.O. will want to see it—he'll be here in a minute.'

I bustled about as anxious as he.

'Then let's get it re-typed at once. Come on! I'll help you. Sit down. Got some foolscap? Right. I'll read the list out— I can manage to see through the ink. Ready? First, the heading . . .'

'Oh, I know the heading, sir,' he answered, settling down before the typewriter. 'It reads: "List of Pilots".' He began to tap the keys. 'Pilots for Single-seat Fighters . . .' *Tap— tap—tap. Tap-a-tap. Tap.* 'S.E.5, Sopwith Camels and Dolphins.' *Tap—tap—tap.* ' "Name and Rank".' *Tap-tap-a-tap.* 'Now, sir, if you please?'

'Yes, what is it?'

'The first name, please, sir.'

'The first name?'

'Yes, sir, the first.'

Mine is a difficult name to catch. I spelled it out carefully. *Tap-tap. Tap-a-tap. Tap-tap. . . .*

After an early lunch a Crossley tender bore me off in the direction of the front. I was sorry for those who had been waiting for nearly three weeks, but then I had been waiting for nearly three years.

F*

5

Wings of Victory

I

Those drivers of Crossley tenders who ferried air-pilots across
northern France always seemed to me a most mysterious lot
of men. Their knowledge of the country, of the roads and
byroads—some of which I was never able to find again—
smacked of the supernatural. The way in which they drove,
unerringly and in silence, direct to squadrons of whose
location, of whose very numbers the passengers were ignorant
attained to the miraculous. They were a race of men apart,
inscrutable, possessed of a knowledge beyond our divination;
for while they carried us behind them they were the sole
arbiters of our chosen destiny. There was an uncanny family
likeness about all of them, particularly in the set of the jaw.

A curious similarity, too, linked my first journey to this
my second. True, the first commencing in St Omer had ended
after a halt at Aire, upon the banks of the Lys, whereas
the second took me from Berck to south of Doullens.
(And there is a world of difference between Flanders and
Picardy.) But there were other close resemblances, close
enough to bring back memories of what seemed a long-
forgotten war in a bygone century. It was, in fact, within a
month of three years since I had last approached the front
in a Crossley tender. The season, the weather were almost the
same. The roads, winding over undulating fields or rushing
straight down long tree-lined avenues, were white and dusty.
Lorries were more plentiful, and ambulances and staff cars,
but horse transport was still in evidence. There were still
farm-carts on the roads, and wagons laden with hay. There
were still peasants in blue smocks and wooden shoes in the

fields, cattle in the farmyards, women at the doors, and smoke from old chimneys. France in the back areas had not, I fancied, changed much in a hundred years—although no doubt Corot would have been surprised to find his dancing nymphs replaced among the poplars in the meadows by Chinese coolies.

But the lack of change behind the lines made me wonder again whether I had not imagined the period of captivity. It was hard to realise that I had been absent during the immensity of those years between. So many men—millions of them!—had marched down these same roads since I had passed by. Day and night for a thousand days the guns had muttered behind the horizon to the east, rising to thunder during those incredible battles—the Somme, Arras, Messines, Ypres, Cambrai and the great German attack. Had I really missed so much? I could scarcely believe it, could scarcely credit that battalions, divisions, armies of men had vanished, that a score of young men whom I had known intimately —at school, in the infantry, in the Flying Corps—had no longer a voice in that everlasting clamour of war a few miles away. I was not 'coming back'; it was into another war that I was being drawn, as though I myself had been killed during the Long Reconnaissance on that blustering December day in 1915, to be reincarnated, after an uneasy stretch in purgatory, amid surroundings familiar enough but amongst men unknown to me. Not one of the half-dozen pilots in the tender knew anyone I knew, and they spoke of squadrons and their histories with an ease that left me silent and alone with my memories.

They left the tender, those six pilots, at various points along the road where squadrons had their headquarters, until at length I was the only one remaining behind the taciturn driver. That, too, was just as three years before. I found my-self wondering to what sort of a temporary home I was being driven. Would I meet with the same chilling reception as in the barge? Would I find a Starched Shirt in command, a Growl to insist upon salutes and standings to attention, a Foxy to make me feel 'all goosey'? I was very much afraid that my history might repeat itself far too accurately.

We came to a farm, turned off the main road, bumped over the ruts of a winding track. My head began to nod, for the drive had been long and the evening was warm. When, after one exceptionally long doze, I opened my eyes, I saw a line of poplars and thought myself back upon the Lys. . . . But there was no river here; a wide expanse of open field was spread before the poplars, themselves bordering a wood upon the brow of a low hill. There were canvas sheds at the side of the field, two groups of them with the usual adjuncts of transport lorries, workshops, store tents. We passed the first group—I had already begun to collect my belongings, but the driver shook his head—and driving round the aerodrome went slowly down a lane between the second group of sheds and the small, dense wood. At a gate leading into an orchard we came to a halt.

'Here you are, sir,' the driver announced, speaking to me for the first time while, with a stub of pencil, he ticked my name off the list. 'This is your squadron. Name of the place? Valheureux.'

I got down. The driver hailed a couple of men near one of the sheds to help unload my kit, and I turned away to advance reluctantly through the gate into the orchard, wishing I had one of my prison friends with me. Now that I had arrived I positively dreaded the first moments in a strange mess with strange pilots.

My feet lagged in spite of the necessity to go forward—under the eyes of the tender-driver I could not turn back—and I had time to look about me at scattered tents and small huts, the grass was growing long between them. Ahead of me, half-hidden by apple trees, was a large mess-tent connected by a short canvas passageway to a wooden building rather like a cricket pavilion. It was painted green and had small lattice windows, a sloping roof and a wooden porch along the front. Evidently the mess. A comfortable looking place, snug and homelike, tucked away amid the trees and lush grass. I hoped devoutly that the inmates would not turn out to be unbearable. . . .

A voice called to me from the porch; a young pilot, whom I recognised as one I had known in England, rose from a camp-chair and hurried towards me as I looked hesitatingly around.

'I'm awfully glad to see you—what luck your coming here! I didn't think you would get out to France for months yet.

How did you do it? Come on into the mess. I'll show you round the squadron presently. . . .'

As a first step I could not have wished for better. To be greeted as an old friend by someone, to be told that he was 'awfully glad' to see me was just the tonic I needed. Confidence began to return with the first sip.

On the porch I met and shook hands with two pilots, both friendly and both Americans: Larry Bowen and Johnny Speaks, and then my friend led me into the main room of the pavilion. It was empty just then, so that I was able to get my bearings before meeting the rest of the squadron.

'I say, do you realise what squadron this is?' my friend went on—the corruption of his name most generally used in the squadron was Shutters.* 'You're in luck to be sent here. This is the most famous scout squadron in France— Ball was in it, and McCudden, and Rhys Davies, Gerald Maxwell and a flock of others. . . .'

I thought of a dark, stone-vaulted room in a German prison and of a Scottish pilot, recently captured, telling me of the squadrons and the airmen in France: 'the best of the bunch—Captain Ball. . . .' That pilot had been taken at the close of the winter's fighting on the Somme. Now, of a sudden, it seemed that no time at all had passed since I had heard him speak. Prison—the Somme and Cambrai—the concentrated efforts to escape—the Dutch frontier—and so to France, to Ball's squadron: it was the only logical sequence. Once more the army was attacking, past the ruins of the Somme, on towards Cambrai and St Quentin and the Hindenburg Line. The enemy had been held, repulsed, was at length being forced back. I was ready to play my own small part in the air again. But Captain Ball was dead. . . .

Shutters went on.

'And do you know that this squadron has brought down more German machines than any other in France! Look at that list of honours!'

He pointed to the far wall. Beneath a wooden propeller of German make and between two black canvas crosses cut from an enemy aircraft, a three-ply board was fixed in a carved

* Derived from an absent-minded habit of keeping radiator-shutters closed during the climb, causing his engine to overheat, with unhappy results.

wooden frame. The number of the squadron was at the head: below were the names of men who had won decorations.

Bravery, I suppose, is relative like everything else and the displaying of it in such a manner as to earn a decoration must generally be a matter of chance; yet in this squadron the number of awards and the period over which they were spread under successive commanders seemed to prove beyond doubt that the work of its pilots had been consistently courageous. Ball headed the list. The date against his name was June 6th, 1917. From that date until my arrival a year and three months had passed, and in that time the members of the squadron had collected two V.C.s, six D.S.O.s. fourteen M.C.s, eight bars to M.C.s, and six D.F.C.s. . . . I remember laughing out loud as I looked at that long list—much to Shutters' surprise.

'What's the matter?' he demanded rather crossly. 'Aren't there enough names there?'

'Oh, yes—almost too many. I was thinking of the squadron I belonged to in 1915. There we had one M.C. between the whole lot of us. It would have been funny to have seen that lonely name on a board in the barge!'

'Perhaps you didn't have the same opportunities in those days,' Shutters was kind enough to remark. 'Who was your C.O.?'

'The Starched Shirt,' I told him, giving the name.

'Never heard of him,' murmured Shutters. And somehow I found his answer full of meaning; the Starched Shirt was a general now, in charge of training or something, a successful senior officer, not a bad fellow at heart, and fond of Surtees I recalled. Yet the younger generation of war pilots had 'never heard of him'. But these men—these names headed by that of 'Captain Ball, V.C., D.S.O., M.C., Légion d'Honneur'—they would not soon be forgotten by those who fought. Indeed the final and greatest Decoration to which so many had already attained would ensure that their names lived on for evermore. So that on joining such a squadron and seeing such a list for the first time one might well believe oneself to be standing at a parting of the ways; the way of the excellent Starched Shirts of this world, or the way of Ball, Rhys Davies, McCudden and others.

A Gilbertian verse tugged my memory:

'Is life a boon?
If so, it must befall
That death, whene'er he call,
Must call too soon!'

Too soon? I forgot about the squadron on the banks of
the Lys, and read slowly through the names on my new
squadron's roll of honour. . . .

'Let's go down to the sheds,' said Shutters impatiently.

II

On my way back from the aerodrome I met the C.O. for
the first time. I was following Shutters along a narrow path
through the orchard, when he came out from a trim wooden
hut amid the trees. Shutters stopped and saluted. I did likewise.

'Hullo—what's the game?' said the major. He was tall,
lean, young; his small moustache seemed almost black by
contrast with his exceedingly pale face. He wore the uniform
of the 9th Lancers, Wings, and a Military Cross ribbon.

'New pilot, sir, just arrived,' Shutters announced. And
then like an ass he added, after mentioning my name: 'He's
an escaped prisoner.'

The major smiled, but I could see at once that he was
scared. He evidently remembered something about the authorities' attitude to prisoners. His questions were asked in a
mild manner, but quickly and to the point. Where had I
served before—when had I been captured—when escaped?

'Good Lord—I suppose it's all right?' he exclaimed at the
end.

'Oh, perfectly all right, sir,' I answered airily. 'I've fixed
it all up with the Air Ministry.'

He was silent, and for a moment I was horrified by the
thought that he was going to announce his intention of
making inquiries. Then his smile broadened. He did not
speak, but I seem to read the word 'Liar!' in his eyes. And I
smiled back at him, for I felt sure it was a friendly reproach.

'Well, I suppose you're anxious to get some of your own

back,' he said at length. 'I expect you've got a score or two to pay off?'

I told him that that was my main idea in returning and that I should like to start as soon as possible.

'Oh, there's plenty of time,' he replied. 'Besides, it's a rule that new pilots don't go over the lines until they've been three weeks with the squadron.'

Three weeks! I protested in alarm. In three weeks anything might happen. I wanted to get going at once. I had been over the lines before—that must be obvious or I would not have been captured—I had plenty of flying-hours to my credit, experience with S.E.5s and so on. The major went on smiling.

'I dare say I might make an exception in your case,' he conceded as he turned away towards the sheds. 'You'll have to do some formation and firing practice first though. You don't want to be shot down the first time you go on patrol over the lines!'

III

It was getting late. Shutters and I strolled back to the mess where already most of the pilots had gathered for cocktails. The majority were very young—that is, few of them were any older than myself and few wore decorations, for the squadron had had heavy losses in the past month or two. I will not claim that I was welcomed like a long lost friend, because I did not know any of them by sight or by name, but there was a hint of geniality about their greeting that put me at ease. At first I was more diffident than they were, since, with memories of my first night in the barge, I rather expected to be given the cold shoulder, but with the arrival of a round of drinks what little ice there was melted rapidly.

Everyone was in good spirits. Two German machines had been shot down that morning. The squadron's total bag since coming to France was nearing the four hundred mark—an average of almost one a day over a period of more than a year! Of course, things were slowing up because the older German aircraft over which the S.E.5s of the squadron had had an undoubted superiority were being replaced by more efficient machines. The Fokker D VII biplane was the principal enemy to be fought now, and against that good little machine the S.E. had to be careful. 'Dive and zoom,' I was told, 'dive and zoom—don't try a dog-fight with them until you've had plenty of experience. They can generally out-manœuvre you.'

'But we're faster on the level and in a dive,' said the American Larry Bowen. 'Keep the old S.E. going fast and you can beat anything in the sky.'

'Yes, but those darned Fokkers can outclimb us,' put in a Canadian flight-commander. 'The best thing to do is to get height at the beginning of the patrol, between eighteen and twenty thousand feet, manœuvre for the sun—then, when you see your Huns, half-roll and dive on to their tails.'

'And keep going,' Larry repeated. 'Don't stop to argue unless you're mighty sure of yourself—just dive straight through them and zoom up later to see what's left. Then you can half-roll and dive again. . . .'

I was back in France! In a famous and efficient fighting squadron whose pilots were still eager and ready to add to their laurels. Their feelings, their desires, their ideals were also mine. There was no cold water to quench enthusiasm here. To the younger pilots I might appear as something of a curiosity, a sort of Rip van Winkle of the air who compared all that they told of modern fighting with conditions existing in 1915; but they soon realised I was keener on flying than on talking about the past, which was all that really mattered to them. And to me their old-new jargon spoken within sound of the guns was very thrilling.

Presently 'Gilly' came into the mess. Gilly was the name of the C.O., though not, of course, used to his face. I had not noticed any particular stiffness about him at the first meeting, but now, the day's work over, he seemed to have unbent completely.

'Well, chaps, how about it? A slight celebration tonight I think,' were his first exclamations. 'Now then, where's the Newt?' The 'Newt', I discovered later, was the diminutive adjutant. 'Newt, go and tell the band to fall in here at once. And—where's that mess-corporal?—Corporal, ask the officers what they want to drink . . .'

A band? I watched the six members of the orchestra file in by a side door past the small bar and pantry. A piano stood in a corner of the room; drums, fiddles, a double-bass gathered round it—men of the squadron, led by a broad-shouldered moustachioed sergeant with a violin.

'Strike up!' ordered Gilly. 'And start off with the squadron tune.'

To some it might make pleasant reading were I able to record that, with the squadron-commander and his gallant officers standing stiffly to attention, the orchestra played a selection from 'Pomp and Circumstance', beginning with a noble and full-throated chorus of 'Land of Hope and Glory'. Or perhaps, with Americans present, 'The Star-Spangled Banner' would have been appropriate. . . . The melody chosen by the squadron to which I now had the honour to belong could only, I am afraid, be regarded as frivolous. It was called 'The Darktown Strutters' Ball', and the first line of its refrain informed some unnamed lady that: 'I'll be there to get you in a taxi, honey.' But nobody worried about the words and the rhythm was invigorating. It was—it is—a damn' good tune! And the orchestra played wonderfully well, superbly I thought. It may have been the cocktails, but I began to bless the good fortune which had brought me to this happy squadron.

After dinner Gilly, solemn for the moment, read out the names of those going on the Dawn Patrol. I was foolishly disappointed to find that my own name was not amongst them.

IV

On the way to my tent that night I made a detour through the orchard so as to come out into the open on the eastern side of the aerodrome. I was impelled by some strange excitement—not alcoholic!—to see what was happening in the direction of the front lines.

It was a dark night, but the horizon was aglow with intermittent gun flashes. We were too far from the retiring line of battle for me to see the flares sent up from the trenches, but their wavering light shone from behind the skyline with unearthly effect, as if playful giants were striking box after box of titanic matches. Owing to the recent German defeats the distance to the front was nearly fifteen miles, so that the sounds reaching me were softened and confused. A continual vague rumour kept the night alive, occasionally a long burst of machine-gun fire would rise and fall as though borne upon an impalpable breeze, but in the main it was the thudding of the guns which alone was plainly audible, the flashes which gave the scene reality.

Gun-fire held, for me that night, the utmost significance. The last time the sound had come to my ears from the front in France I had stood peering *westwards* from the window of a prison camp in the Saar. Now I faced over open ground— to the east!

From between the orchard trees at my back came the strains of the orchestra playing the final piece of the evening: the squadron's tune, 'Tomorrow night at the Darktown Strutters' Ball.' Tomorrow—I would fly again in France. Only a practice flight, but with what meaning for me! The squadron lay not far from the Somme battlefields. I would fly to the neighbourhood of Bapaume, fly over the very place where I had landed to become a prisoner.

V

It was actually something like ten days before I was allowed to cross the lines officially. I say 'officially' because of course I could not resist the temptation to sneak across during various practice flights; but not too far over, for I was mortally afraid of displeasing my new squadron-commander before I had had time to achieve anything. Gilly was willing to let me take my full share of the squadron's work as soon as possible, but he was right in holding me back. It would have been very awkward, when some of the Air Ministry officials concerned were not even aware of my presence in France, had I disappeared or been recaptured on my first flight.

Every day I was allowed to take up an S.E., either for formation flying or for firing practice at a ground target, so that gradually I became more confident of doing my share alongside those pilots whose experience seemed, at first, so much greater than any I could hope to acquire. Firing at a ground target was good practice for attacks on trenches and troops as well as for aerial combats, and with hints and tips from Gilly himself I began to learn something of both forms of fighting. The squadron was now frequently employed on operations such as aerodrome raids, bombing of troops and transport and harassing tactics generally, in addition to its normal occupation of high altitude fighting; for the ebb and flow which, since the German offensive in March, had come into the hitherto stagnant position-war had greatly increased the importance of guerilla attacks by fast single-seaters. 'Risky work,' I was told, 'but well worth it.' Later on indeed these operations became of such value as to out-weigh by far the bringing down of a few more enemy aero-planes.

Meanwhile it was our business to be ready for both jobs and I took the firing practice seriously, believing that, as Gilly had said, there would be plenty of time to pay off old scores. I had waited for so long, a little more patience was easy to command. The war would slow down during the winter months whilst I gained experience; in the spring and early summer I would be ready for the final victories.

Casualties, however, brought suddenly nearer the day when I was to be sent off to measure my skill and my luck. A flight-commander was wounded not many days after my arrival; then a young pilot was reported missing, a third fell ill and was taken to hospital. Not heavy losses, but persistent enough to make replacement necessary even by such novices as myself. An aerodrome raid—upon Estourmel, at which I was a mere spectator, high up in the sky with the protective flight —was hailed as a success, but it cost the life of the young American Larry Bowen. And then another pilot was reported missing. . . .

And thus stepping into dead men's shoes—or more accur-ately into the cockpit of a vanished pilot—I found my name one evening at the tail end of the list for the Dawn Patrol.

VI

That Chance which, alternately good and evil, had steered my course throughout the war now showed itself clearly.

For with that very first Dawn Patrol my carefully laid plans were blown to pieces as though they had been struck by a direct hit from an Archie shell, and I became involved in a whirlwind of events which did not cease blowing until the war itself ended.

And yet the day began in a normal manner. We left the aerodrome in the grey light, taking off in formation and flying east into the brilliant sky of a perfect morning, climbing steadily to cross the lines south-west of Cambrai and head for the rising sun, testing our guns as we went. Below us lay the ruined country of which not even Sir Thomas Browne could have said that it had survived the drums and tramplings of three conquests. On both sides the artillery was busy, presaging a heavy day in the air. Presently Archie opened up on us, keeping his usual fairly safe distance so that I rejoiced to hear the old familiar sound of his chronic cough. At eighteen thousand feet we turned north-east, and a few moments later, somewhere above the line Valenciennes-Cambrai, we sighted a large enemy formation.

I say 'we' because I suppose everyone saw the enemy machines at more or less the same time, but actually it didn't much matter whether I sighted them or not. I was the last man on the right of the top, protective flight; it was for the leader of the lower flight to find and attack the enemy—which is what he did. Hardly had I recognised the distinctive silhouette of Fokker biplanes than I saw a red light shoot up from our own leader and down he went in a steep dive to support the lower flight. For a moment it seemed as if the enemy were going to dive too, then his formation broke up, scattered and engaged our machines. This caused our own flights also to break up, each man going after the enemy nearest to him, and in a few seconds, instead of neat 'V's' manœuvring for position, the air was full of machines hurtling in all directions like traffic at a badly regulated street intersection. The, for me, ticklish operation of a dog-fight was in full swing.

'Dive and zoom,' they had told me, so I dived and zoomed. For an instant a Fokker flashed full into my sights; I dived hard, pressed the trigger-release and prayed for victory. But with what seemed no more than a flick of the pilot's wrist he swerved off at right-angles, and a second later shots from another enemy crackled past my head. 'Dive and zoom!' I made haste to obey. 'If the enemy fire is too hot—hard rudder and no bank—side slip!' I tried that too. . . .

All at once I found myself outside the dog-fight. I looked round hastily. Two of the enemy had gone down as the result of our first attack, but already the fight was practially over, with the enemy chasing our people away. 'Attack—dive and zoom . . .' it had been, now it was 'dive for home'. Until we could get clear and re-form the V, it was each man for himself. Fortunately my last zoom had taken me above and away from the main group of the enemy, for having started at the tail-end of the flight, I had been left a considerable distance behind. Opening my engine to full throttle, I pushed the nose down along the shortest course for our lines.

And then, looking about to see that no enemy was sneaking up to get a shot in from astern, I noticed something very odd. The clear blue sky was streaked with condensation, criss-crossed with the smoke of tracer bullets, the thin lines of greyish vapour shining in the bright sunlight. Archie puffs were dotted here and there, and a dark trail showed where a machine had gone down in flames. But there was something else. A thick blue-grey streamer of smoke was festooned over the scene of the recent fight—circling, diving; zooming—following the course of one of the machines engaged. I could see no craft, friendly or hostile, from which this streamer could be coming, but glancing over my shoulder I saw that it became thicker and darker the nearer it came to me. . . . I jerked my head round anxiously. It came from my own machine.

I was not on fire, that was my first joyful thought. The thick oily smoke came from the starboard exhaust pipe, and watching the end of the pipe I saw small pieces of metal come trickling out. Something was very much the matter. I had heard the click and rattle of a couple of shots getting home on the machine at the beginning of the fight, and now that I came to notice it the engine was vibrating a lot, the revolution-counter wavering slowly downwards. I must hurry to recross the lines. I looked over the side to make sure that I was following the best course.

We had gone a long distance east to find the enemy and the usual west wind had carried us still farther during the fight. I had made good headway so far, but as near as I could judge the lines were twelve to fifteen miles away. Cambrai lay beyond my starboard wing tips, below were open fields—a queerly reminiscent stretch of country. I glanced back. Valenciennes showed up unpleasantly close, almost directly under my tail-plane. The altimeter pointed to less than fourteen thousand feet. Fifteen miles to go, against the wind, with a failing engine. . . . I had done all this before! Exactly the same thing over this identical course. Valenciennes, the west wind, engine trouble—it was happening all over again. A bit of history, unimportant to anyone save myself, was bent on repeating itself.

Archie crept close and a cloud passed over the sun. It was so bumpy at low altitudes that I lost height more rapidly. There was heavy fighting going on below, clouds of smoke, and a terrific bombardment; I could hear it plainly above the tired rumble of the engine and the dreary humming of the wires. I was getting close—but I was hearing the guns from the wrong side of the lines. If only the wind would drop. . . .

At three thousand feet the failing engine subsided altogether. I switched off. The bombardment became menacingly loud.

VII

I must suppose that Chance wished to show me the other side of the picture—what might have happened with a bit of luck nearly three years before. Because I landed amid the shell-holes near the village of Quéant, about a mile and a half behind the British front. Somehow or other the machine had managed to drift over the trenches in spite of Archie and I landed her, much to my surprise, without breaking anything. But I was still very worried when I got out of the cockpit; the sensation of being doomed to recapture had been so strong I could not easily shake it off. Anxiously I looked into the cubby-hole behind the pilot's seat to see if the flare for setting her alight was safely stowed. The guns were loud, but even now they seemed to be firing in the wrong direction. I had lost my bearings in the last moments of that uncomfortable glide. . . .

A voice hailed me. I jumped round in alarm. But it was a friendly head which poked itself out of a dugout doorway.

'Come on in,' said the owner of the head. 'Must have been cold up there this morning. Have some whisky!'

I did.

And later I got on the 'phone to the squadron, spoke to the Newt.

'I'll send a tender for you,' he said. 'Glad you're safe, we thought you were missing. Don't forget to bring back the watch!'

The eight-day luminous watch was the one item on the instrument board which appealed to all men. It was easily detachable, so easily that any machine left untended for more than a few minutes was invariably looted of its valuable timepiece. The first thing a pilot had to remember, no matter how serious the crash, was to unscrew the watch. But the morning's events must have unsettled me for I left it in the machine.

The tender arrived at noon and that same evening I dined again in the mess instead of, as I had for a while feared, in St Quentin gaol. The Newt was a little upset at my having forgotten the watch, but Gilly was good enough to say that he was pleased to see me back; he too, it seemed, had had a nasty feeling that I might have been retaken, and I think he knew what the thought of recapture meant to me. That, however, was something more than one of the junior pilots understood. At dinner I happened to sit next to him. He came from somewhere near Glasgow and so was called, I suppose inevitably, Jock.

'What was the major talking about?' he asked. 'Something about your having been a prisoner—surely you were never such a fool as to get captured.?'

I admitted that it was so, that I had been just such a fool.

'But, good God, man—how did you manage it? And you were there *two and a half years?* Unwounded at that? I can't believe it!'

'I'm afraid it's true,' I told him sadly. 'And it really couldn't be helped.'

'Nonsense! No pilot ever needs to be taken prisoner.'

'Supposing it happens to you some day, what then?'

'I'll get back before I'm caught.'

I began to feel uncomfortable—worried for him.

'But if your engine fails when you're, say, fifteen or twenty miles on the wrong side of the lines?'

'I'll glide home.'

'And if the wind is against you and you haven't enough height to glide over the front?'

'Those are absurd suppositions, but if it did happen that I was forced to land in enemy territory I would know what to do.'

'What's that?'

'Run away—hide in a wood—take cover somewhere. And crawl back after dark through the trenches. I'd know how to do it—I've served in the infantry.'

So might I have spoken in the days of the barge on the Lys.

'Well, if you didn't have the luck to do any of those things, you might still be taken prisoner.'

'And be put in a German gaol? Pouf—I'd be out of that before they'd had time to lock the doors!'

Ten days later the Dawn Patrol returned after a sharp engagement with a large number of Fokkers. It was my morning off and I stood on the aerodrome counting the S.E.s as they came in to land. Two were missing. One of them contained Jock.

My sorrow was genuine, for the loss was the squadron's and it seemed probable by all accounts that Jock had been killed. But before the end of the week we heard that he was safe—a prisoner and unwounded. Then, I must confess, I laughed. And I think we all wondered if we should not soon see him back, a free man after breaking gaol and crawling through the lines. Presently we forgot all about him—as they must have forgotten about me on the Lys.

VIII

At some time during the war Rudyard Kipling wrote a number of verses dedicated to various categories of people engaged in the struggle. In a moment of poetic aberration he wrote of a young pilot diving through clouds, 'his milk-teeth yet unshed. . . .' Merciful heavens! we were young, but not that childish and by St Apollina, patron saint of dentists, there were no loose teeth in Gilly's squadron. Think of stopping in the middle of a dog-fight to spit out a couple of pre-molars!

However, even supposing Kipling's picture to have been accurately painted, I would assuredly have lost the whole galaxy on the afternoon of September 28th. I came near to more than that.

'Now then, chaps, a big show today,' Gilly had told us in the morning. 'There's a full-size war in progress—attack on the Hindenburg Line. We do high patrols first, and this afternoon trench-*strafing*. The Boche is taking it in the neck—got to stop his reinforcements coming up and harass his retreat, if any. Now off you go—dive and zoom—and if their fire gets too heavy remember the safest thing is to *keep low down*!'

We left at intervals in flights of three, loaded up with ammunition and four 25-pound bombs apiece. My own party, led by a senior pilot, made for Cambrai, crossed the lines at two thousand feet and began circling the country to the south of the town looking for targets.

There was a great battle going on underneath, to the west of the Scheldt Canal; the air was bumpy with explosions and with the flight of high trajectory shells. Comparatively undamaged country was rapidly being battered to pieces, villages were collapsing like sand castles overwhelmed by the tide, churches went down in clouds of dust, farms and isolated houses blazed furiously. Of course, the main clamour of warfare was inaudible to us above the roaring of our engines and the persistent singing of the wires, so that flying low it was ever surprising to see, without warning sound, a mass of broken earth fly into the air as a heavy shell burst nearby, or to observe a stout wall suddenly collapse in smoke and débris without so much as a murmur having reached one's ears. Rather like a silent film. . . . Few troops were to be seen on the German side and little movement. At first it was hard to find suitable targets, especially since we were flying in formation.

Keeping formation even at high altitudes always bothered me when a scrap was imminent, I suppose because my early training had formed an instinctive desire to be alone and unhampered. Certainly I never learnt to feel comfortable fighting in V-formation and near the ground the proximity of other pilots was to me intolerable. On this occasion our first few dives at small parties of enemy infantry seemed positively feeble, for we were worrying far too much about keeping the right distance from one another, and about pulling out of each dive as soon as the leader did, to aim properly or to fire with any enthusiasm. Moreover, cruising about at some fifteen hundred feet from the ground we were offering an easy target for machine-gunners as well as for Archie. At the first objective worthy of my bombs I decided to break away from the others and work on my own.

Presently my interest was aroused by a small railway station south-east of Cambrai. It seemed at first glance to be deserted, but we had come gradually lower and I happened to notice some half a dozen German soldiers standing motionless beside what must have been the waiting-room. In their field-grey uniforms they were practically invisible and I should never have seen them but for the white circles of their upturned faces. It was funny seeing German faces so close to me again. Like being half-way back to prison. Funny? Well, I didn't exactly hate them, but I disliked them a good deal and this was war; I broke off from the formation, circled round and dropped two bombs.

Since I was not more than a hundred feet up the bombs made a nasty sort of *Clang—Clang!* under my S.E.'s tail, but there was no other response from the ground. When I looked back the signal box was hidden by a cloud of black smoke and there was a big dent in the roof of the waiting-room. . . . So far so good. I searched around for other targets. This was rather fun, I thought, and not too dangerous if one kept as low down as Gilly advised. The trouble was that to put in a reasonably long burst of fire one had to zoom up to about five hundred feet where concentrated rifle and machine-gun fire was apt to become much too hot. However, with a bit of turning, twisting and sideslipping I hoped to counter that.

By this time the other two machines of the flight had vanished, had found other targets I supposed. I was alone again; if I got shot down no one would know where I had gone to. Time enough to think of that later. . . . I found some

Germans in trenches—half-rolled, dived and zoomed. Then a party strolling through a cutting between two hills—dived and zoomed again. I heard them return my fire, but they did no damage, and a few moments later I saw a cart drawn by two horses moving briskly down a road. There were a number of men in the cart—I saw the details clearly as I passed within a hundred feet of them. I don't know what they were doing, whether retiring or going up the front, for the winding road ran approximately parallel to the firing line. But it was a tempting target, and again the sight of those German uniforms gave me an odd sensation of annoyance. I dived from eight hundred feet.

When he heard me coming the man on the box whipped up his horses. Why he did that I cannot say, for there was nowhere for him to go, and it made little difference to me whether his cart travelled fast or slow. I suppose the men in the cart got excited when my first shots fell amongst them, perhaps they yelled. At all events the horses bolted, left the road, the cart tipped over and rolled down a grass bank into a stream. My last glimpse of the man who had been on the box showed me a face strangely reminiscent, at that distance and in that second, of an extremely disagreeable *Feldwebel* at Fort Zorndorf. I felt that I had paid off a score. . . . And when I pulled out of the dive the wires were screaming triumphantly like the blare of brass in the ride of the Valkyries.

I stared ahead. Beyond a line of trees three or four flashes of yellow light winked at me. Guns! Not very well concealed, they had evidently moved up hurriedly. I had two bombs left—just the thing. Approaching from behind the trees, I zoomed up a couple of hundred feet to see what I was doing, and pulled the bomb-release handle. . . .

And then I don't know what happened. Rising instantly above the *clang* of my bomb there came a roar like the ending of the world. Something kicked at the tail of my S.E. lifting it up as if it were paper, throwing the nose down into an almost vertical dive, out of control. . . .

I know that what I am describing sounds incredible, but I also know that it happened, and that men in the squadron, Gilly amongst others, saw the machine afterwards and testified to its condition.

To estimate how long that dive lasted is beyond my powers. Perhaps it was two seconds, probably less. Reckoning that I was travelling at well over a hundred miles an hour and that when the dive started I was three hundred feet up, it must certainly have been less. And yet I had time for coherent thought. No past life flashed before me; my eyes remained open and it was the immediate future I looked into. I saw the ground appallingly close coming up at speed. I felt the control stick rigid in my hand, as hard back as I could get it —but jammed. I thought that I was 'for it'. In those infinite fractions of time I passed through fear, beyond despair, into a bleak region where without hope I *knew* that I was going to dive into the ground.

And so I did.

How it came about that I survived I can only explain in this manner. The machine had come slowly and almost of her own accord out of the vertical, but she was still descending steeply and at great speed when she smashed into the earth. There was a ghastly noise of breaking and splintering, I was flung forward against the safety-belt, my head hit the windscreen; but the machine quivered, bounced, and went on—minus her undercarriage. There must have been a slight fall in the ground just at that point, for had it been level or sloping up I would have crashed irremediably and fatally. As it was the machine seemed to stagger forward, her speed reduced almost to stalling-point; gradually her nose came up until she hovered along a few feet from the ground. She could still fly; by some tiny fraction of time and distance she had missed stopping altogether.

And now fear returned like pain after an operation. Dead certainty of the end had acted as an anaesthetic, returning hope brought new terror. What would happen next? The control stick was impossibly heavy, stiff, something had gone wrong with the tail. I glanced over my shoulder, and sat aghast at what I saw. On one side the fuselage had been stripped bare of its tail-plane and elevator, which now trailed, broken and tattered, at the end of a bracing-wire. The rudder was partially jammed by the wreckage; I could scarcely steer, dared not use too much force on the rudder-bar. The under-carriage, I knew, was gone, but worse than that the tip of a propeller-blade had been carried away. The engine vibration alone was nerve-shattering, and I could only guess what other damage must have been done to the frame-work of the machine. The extraordinary thing was that she flew at all; for the moment that was all I cared about.

By careful manipulation of the engine throttle and of the half-jammed control stick I succeeded in obtaining more or less level flight at an altitude of about one hundred feet. Lateral control was not too bad, but with only half a tail the machine had a horrible tendency to pitch uncontrollably. The best speed, I found, was about eighty miles an hour, and to obtain this I had to run the engine at three-quarters of full throttle, thereby bringing on such a vibration as made me fear the engine would break loose if I did not land soon. But to land in German territory was something that did not occur to me.

The likelihood of a crash was brought home by the attitude of the enemy. I passed over a nest of German machine-gunners. I saw the gun pointed, the men in field-grey crouching behind it. But the gun did not fire. Looking down at them I watched their heads rise, looked into their upturned faces, almost caught the expression of blank surprise in their open-mouthed immobility. They were too startled by my wheel-less, tail-less, rattling machine to think of firing. . . . I overtook a solitary steel-helmeted German walking towards the front. He spun round in alarm when he heard me coming, bent down to take cover; then slowly straightened up and stood regarding me, legs apart, as I passed unsteadily on my way. It was the same with the rest of them. The enemy did not think it worth their while to waste ammunition on a doomed and harmless craft.

I had been heading almost due north at the moment of impact and, although I could not see much of the country when I came out of the dive, I knew enough to realise that I was making for Cambrai and not for the lines. With infinite care I pressed the rudder-bar to bring the nose round from north-east, through north, to north-west. More than this I dared not attempt, for the remains of the tail were now vibrating as much as the engine; greater pressure on the rudder might bring about a final collapse. But in a little while, clearing some treetops by a few feet, I saw the Scheldt Canal go by beneath me. It was the first reassuring sign since the crash and it gave me confidence to continue, though by now I was as frightened of coming down as of staying up, knowing that I would have practically no control of the machine on landing.

Then I began to see the *backs* of Germans in trenches, in shell-holes, behind mounds and in the ruins of houses. The earth started to spout broken fountains of mud, earth, stones. Clouds of smoke rolled by, whilst above the banging of my engine I could hear the deep shuddering boom of guns. It took an age to cross the battle-zone, and all at once I noticed that I was getting much lower. Less than fifty feet from the ground. More like twenty. I tried to climb a little. Impossible. The machine lost speed at once, . . . There was a hill ahead of me—a well-known hill, wood, village: Bourlon! Our people had attacked it that same morning. Question was, had they taken it? If so I might be safe yet. . . . The ground came closer.

I began to see faces, not backs, in the trenches and shell-holes. Dimly through the smoke, I distinguished khaki uniforms. The shell-fire was less heavy. Ahead a gun flashed in my face, firing in the direction whence I had come. The ground drew still nearer, so near that had I possessed an undercarriage the wheels must already have been rolling upon the pitted earth where dead men lay as well in khaki as in field-grey. I tried to pull the nose up, got the speed to just below eighty, switched off; slithered along the ground, hit the rim of a small crater. There was a final crashing and splintering, from the wings this time, and the machine burying her engine in the ground thumped over on to her back.

IX

When I came to, a few seconds later, I was being hauled out of the wreckage by a couple of burly private soldiers. An officer with a very red face stood by, directing operations as though he were assisting at a rather uninteresting bit of salvage work.

'Blimey, sir,' said one of the men, 'look at all the berlood!'

That remark brought me round. I struggled to my feet, anxious to find out where I had been hit. The officer hurried forward solicitously.

'Are you wounded?'

Then if ever I should have quoted Browning: 'Smiling, the youth fell dead. . . .' I was too slow. It was the private soldier who answered for me.

'Garn, sir, it's only 'is nose what's bleedin'!'

The place where I had landed (in a manner of speaking) had been captured an hour previously, so that I had timed my descent rather well. The hill-side was no longer under rifle fire, and the fact that it was being shelled at odd intervals was not sufficient to deter the rank and file; a crowd of idlers soon collected such as, in peace time, assemble to watch a city street being taken up. Through the midst of them there hurried presently a dapper gunner subaltern. He clicked his heels and flung me a salute that would have shamed the guards at Buckingham Palace.

'Battery-commander's compliments, sir, and if you wish for assistance we shall be happy to do anything in our power.' He saluted again.

'Thanks,' I said, holding my nose and feeling very giddy. 'But why the "sir" business and all this saluting?'

It had been a warm day and I was not wearing flying-kit over my uniform. I saw him glance down in a puzzled manner at the badges on my sleeve, and when he spoke again it was in a much less humble tone.

'Oh—I thought you were at least a wing-commander. You had such a very big streamer on your machine.'

'Streamer be blowed!' said I. 'That was my tail-plane.'

I went on to tell him of some of the peculiar things which had befallen me, thinking that being a gunner he might be able to find an explanation for my having been blown up. But he was listless from the start and at the end plainly disappointed.

'The battery-commander thought you were flying a new type of machine—very fast, without the wheels, don't you know. . . .'

I left him gazing at my wrecked aeroplane, and walked back to the balloon line where they gave me a much-needed whisky-and-soda. Then, finding a tender returning empty to

Schweinhund—the author in his S.E.5a. Photograph taken after the Armistice, with Lewis gun and mounting removed from top plane

Fifty years on. Author with S.E.5a at the Royal Aircraft Establishment, Farnborough, 1968 (*Daily Telegraph*)

the depot, I hopped on board and was driven back to the squadron by easy stages.

X

'We were afraid you had "gone west", sir,' said the clerk in the squadron office when I arrived after dark. 'The returns are all ready to go off to the wing. Another half-hour and you'd have been reported missing.'

He seemed rather disappointed at having to make out a new return.

I made my way to the mess, where Gilly and his officers were at dinner in the big tent. It was a calm night, and I remember noticing how few sounds issued from the open flap through which a broad shaft of light came to colour the stems of the apple trees and chase the shadows through the long grass. The pilots seemed unusually silent. Considering who was believed to be missing, I was surprised and rather gratified that free champagne had not been served out nor the orchestra called in. But on approaching the entrance I was overwhelmed by a stupid self-consciousness. I was beginning to feel tired and incapable of giving lengthy explanations of the day's happenings. I would far sooner have met just one pilot on my way to bed: 'Hullo, so you're back?' —'Yes, I'm back.' He would have spread the news and I could have told them all about it in the morning. However, I was hungry as well as tired. There was nothing for it but to go on.

As I came into the tent I could hear one of the pilots talking to Gilly about the results of the afternoon raid. Suddenly Shutters, who was nearest the entrance, called out: 'Good God—here he is!'

There fell immediately the sort of silence which makes superstitious people observe that it must be twenty-minutes-past or twenty-minutes-to, while all heads were turned anxiously as though to look at an unwelcome ghost. Not knowing exactly what was expected of me, I advanced to the head of the table where Gilly sat. The usual formula employed on entering a mess after dinner has started came to my mind.

G

'I'm sorry I'm late, sir,' I said and was astonished to hear them all laugh.

'What happened?' Gilly asked.

I began to make as good a story as I might out of the adventure, and, fortified with a drink, I was just warming up to the nerve-racking climax when an abrupt question fell like ice upon my conscience.

'Did you remember to bring back the watch?' asked the Newt.

Amid further laughter I turned away, sat down in a quiet corner. I had forgotten the thing again!

XI

Perhaps it was a stubborn desire to bring back at least a watch from future engagements which made me so anxious to start again at once. Certainly Gilly was not keen that I should indulge in any more low raids until I had recovered from the shock of the first. But I did not then understand why he should insist so firmly upon my having a rest; I felt none the worse for my adventure, and I would not admit even to myself that I had had more than a bad scare. It was not until afterwards that I understood the wisdom of Gilly's decision. He knew well the sort of thing likely to affect a pilot's nerves, and how a strain upon those nerves, unless cared for in the right way and in time, may become so serious as to break even the best of health. Gilly knew, because his own health was strained to breaking-point.

He had started the war in German South-West Africa, and had followed it up with a long record of service in France. As a result of one of his aerial combats, he had suffered a serious crash, but on recovering he had insisted on flying at once and, as it turned out, much too soon. He was never really strong again, and hard work as a squadron-commander had worn down his resistance. Nevertheless, on any important raid or at any time when the squadron required experienced leadership he was the keenest man in the air. And I must emphasise that by saying that it was no part of a squadron-commander's duties to fly; on the contrary, organisation generally required his presence on the ground.

To a pilot with bad nerves and in poor health the excitement
and strain of aerial fighting generally and of ground attacks
in particular were very great. On returning from the aerodrome raid in which Larry Bowen was killed, Gilly, who had
been the enthusiastic promoter and leader of the whole show,
landed successfully, taxied up to the sheds, and remained
sitting motionless. Mechanics ran up to find him white as a
sheet. . . . Upon another occasion he had to be helped out of
the cockpit after a fight, and much later he confided to me
that once he had nearly blacked out during a ground attack.

But he refused to give up. His was the sort of courage
that, however hackneyed the word, can only be termed
indomitable. For the sake of the squadron, for the sake of
us, his pilots, he was determined to stick it out—at any rate
until the winter, when, he had been told, the squadron would
return to England to be equipped with a newer and faster
type of machine. Then rested, practised, reorganised, we
would return in greater strength than ever to take part in
the final victory. . . . In his lighthearted way he kept us all
in order; warm in his praise of anything that, in our daily
flying and fighting, accorded with the spirit and traditions
of the squadron. On the evening of some day's achievement
in the air he would order in the orchestra to celebrate or else
bundle us into tenders and carry us off to the nearest town
for dinner. Once we went as far as Dieppe, orchestra and all,
in search of entertainment, returning in the small hours to
wobble into the air in erratic formation. Any adventurous
scheme for annoying the enemy won his approbation, and
he himself was continuously seeking fresh methods of prod-
ding the Germans.

I had the good fortune to see one example of Gilly's
work at very close quarters. In fact, I couldn't well have
been closer. It happened—as far as I can make out from the
tattered leaves of my Combat Reports—on October 8th, on
which day Gilly honoured me with an invitation to go and
shoot down a balloon with him.

But before that a number of incidents had occurred
combining to give me a certain footing in the squadron
as one likely to survive more by luck than by judgment.

For the first few days after my 'tail-less' crash I was sent
off quietly on patrol in formation with the rest of the squadron.

We had one or two fights, but nothing memorable in the way of victories, enemy aircraft just then being rather scarce on our sector of the front. On October 3rd trench-*strafing* began again, and for a while all went well. We found plenty of good targets for bombs as well as for machine-guns, so that the war seemed, from our point of view, to be going on at a rattling good pace. . . . On the 5th I shot down a balloon in flames, and scored a direct hit on a train in Busigny station—Busigny, through which I had steamed miserably in December, 1915, on my way to Germany. Later in the same day I dropped other small bombs, this time on some infantry who were showing their resentment at my presence, and finished up with five hundred rounds of rapid fire into an old archway in Cambrai where a company of Germans were misguidedly sheltering. A good day—but the next was nearly disastrous.

It was my fault this time. I tried too many conclusions with ground machine-guns, which I had foolishly thought could be mastered with a few steep, hard-firing dives. The success of the last days led me to take risks such as I would normally have had the sense to avoid; instead of diving swiftly once or twice and making that quick escape—flat along the ground, round corners of houses, behind trees, following the contours—I allowed myself to get annoyed with the tenacity of some German soldiers. Forgetting all my valuable lessons, I went on diving as though at practice upon an aerodrome target, until one of the nests which I had not been able to silence registered mortal wounds upon my poor S.E.

There had been the usual *crack-crack* of machine-gun bullets all through the engagement, but as I was zooming away from my last dive, ready to half-roll and attack again, the angry little sounds became much louder. Within three seconds I saw a group of holes appear on the left lower wing, a splinter flew off an interplane strut, a flying-wire broke with a twang like that of a bass fiddle. I tried sideslipping, but they held their aim. The fuselage began to rattle like a can of dry peas, something kicked the rudder almost away from my feet—and an instant later a hard *smack!* and a stream of petrol in my face told me that the main tank had been hit.

Frightened of fire more than of anything else, but also of

the next shot which I felt would get me personally, I made for home. The gravity tank was hit too, but there was enough in it to carry me, helped by the height I had gained on the zoom, to safety a mile or so beyond the lines.

They certainly knew how to hit back, those German machine-gunners. There was no scaring them away from their posts; you had to lay them out flat before they would give in. There had been three nests of them that morning, skilfully disposed about the outskirts of a village, covering the retreat of the infantry. I had knocked out the first two—seen the gunners fall, seen new men take their places, seen them fall too, seen one of the guns overturn—but the third, concealed in the ruins of a farmhouse, had given as much as he had received. My machine was more or less of a wreck when I landed.

XII

'I say, if you don't look out you'll get what's coming to you!' Shutters informed me upon the following day.

I was back at the squadron, tuning up the new machine allotted to me and painting her name—*Schweinhund*—upon the three-ply panel below the engine. I can't remember exactly why I chose this name, except that I had been called it more than once and that now most of my work was being done at an altitude where the Germans could read it plainly. ... Shutters' remark was disturbing. I was beginning to think that if the enemy had not recaptured me so far they were not likely to succeed in the future. But such an observation was discouraging, and I told him so.

'Oh, I don't mean that you'll "go west",' he answered quickly. 'I mean you'll be getting your name on the squadron board—collect a D.F.C. or something.'

That brought me up with a jolt. My name on the board at the end of that long list? I had not seriously considered the possibility since coming to the squadron, having been far too busy for such delightful day-dreaming. Moreover I was too much impressed with the achievements of my predecessors to think that either decorations or promotion would ever come my way, certainly not until many hard

months of flying and fighting had passed. Once long ago
in the barge, I had dreamed of these things, and capture
had been the only result. Later on, I think I had a sneaking
feeling that there might be something to be had on my return
from captivity, but as no one had ever suggested anything
so pleasant I had soon forgotten all about it.

And now came Shutters to recall silly boyish hopes of
honour and glory, childish longings for distinctions such as,
I suppose, we all have. I wondered if he could have heard
anything from Gilly, in a roundabout way. Was it possible
that my name was being mentioned 'behind my back', in a
pleasanter manner than that phrase usually implies? I hardly
dared to hope so. I had been with the squadron for so short
a time and, although enemy machines had been brought down
when I had been on patrol, I could claim none of them for
my own. As for my trench-*strafing* work, it did not really
amount to much, and the fairly successful performances of the
past few days had not been reliably witnessed. No 'confirmation' was obtainable.

That word 'confirmation'—which on first hearing I had
mistaken for a religious ceremony—sounded the knell of
many a young pilot's hopes of glory. Coming back from
some furious fight a machine would land, the pilot jump out
and report enthusiastically: 'By Jove—had the hell of a
scrap! Got two Huns down in flames!' To which would
come the chilling reply: 'Can you get confirmation of that?'
It was just as well: optimistic hopes of victory have led us
all a good deal farther than the facts at one time or another.
Personally I had not hitherto been much interested in
'confirmation'; I had, to pursue the analogy, my own private
communion with the enemy—or rather, my personal ven-
detta to satisfy. Given an aeroplane and ammunition I
needed no endorsement on my Combat Reports to make me
happy. But the authorities had to be considered, and, more
important, the record of the squadron.

While Shutters was still trying to persuade me that a
decoration was something more than an extremely remote
possibility, Gilly came down from the squadron office and
strolled up to my machine.

'Hullo—why the paintwork? And what does that name
mean?'

I tried to explain that it was meant to be a bit of 'frightfulness' to annoy the Germans, and that in addition I hoped soon to have sketched out a portrait of the Kaiser on the radiator, painted so that when the shutters were opened and closed rapidly, the Imperial moustaches would wiggle and the eyes blink—the idea being that a picture of the All Highest might put the enemy machine-gunners off their aim. But Gilly did not seem altogether pleased.

'Don't you know there's an order against the painting of machines?' he said. 'And, by the way, the general wants to see you.'

'Good Lord!—shall I rub out the "*Schweinhund*" at once?' I asked nervously, for in those days when a senior officer wanted to see me it was usually to complain about something.

'No, you needn't worry,' Gilly reassured me. 'He doesn't want to see you about that. He wants to confirm you—'

'Is he a bishop?'

'Don't be silly! He wants to confirm your report of yesterday—your attacks on those machine-gun nests.'

'But how the deuce can he do that?'

'Well, it seems he was up visiting the balloon line. And for some odd reason he decided to go up in one of the balloons. While sitting up there admiring the view, he saw an S.E. diving at the village you mention in your report. When the machine came back he saw the squadron markings on it. . . .'

I scarcely listened to the rest of the tale. It sounded like a yarn from another war: Edward III in his windmill watching the Black Prince at Crécy—Napoleon 'upon a little hill'. . . . What luck! To have a real, live general watching the arena and the *morituri* and putting in a favourable report about it! Perhaps, after all, that Squadron Honours board . . .

'And there's another thing,' said Gilly as we parted. 'I want you to take command of your flight from today. . . .'

XIII

Next day Gilly's balloon *strafe* took place.

Our objectives were two observation balloons operating

to the south-east of Cambrai. The enemy, beaten all along the line, was still holding obstinately to that town and to the country south, protected by the remains of his trench system and by the Scheldt Canal—as yet, with all bridges broken, impassable for cavalry or tanks. In this salient fighting continued fiercely, the Germans in force, their machine-gunners valiant, with orders to hold up our advance at all costs. But reinforcements were reaching them with difficulty; artillery searched their back areas, aircraft of all types—heavy bombers or single-seaters, flying high or low, near to or far from the front—were busy destroying communications. Enemy supplies were running low, for they had lost a tremendous amount of material during the past two months' fighting. Even observation balloons were becoming scarce. And that was where Gilly's scheme came in.

It had been observed that the balloon which I had shot down had not been replaced, nor had one to the north of Cambrai which had been seen coming down in flames a few days previously; many others had been withdrawn from more distant parts of the line where the war of movement was getting under way. In the Cambrai salient only two remained in daily use, evidently doing important work observing the gathering mass of our attack and directing fire upon the Scheldt. The Germans took the greatest care of these two balloons, probably because they could get no spares, and at the first warning of danger hauled them down at a truly astonishing speed whilst every gun in the neighbourhood opened up—Archie, machine-guns, 'flaming onions', rifles, even anti-tank guns. Several of our people had tried to attack these balloons when returning from high patrols, but with no result other than to make the enemy more wary. The only chance of success lay in a direct attack, at a comparatively low altitude, from straight across the lines, so as to surprise them in the air before they had time to go down.

Gilly's plan was simple. In the early afternoon a strong flight of the squadron was to cross the lines carrying bombs. They were to look for targets and later descend to attack troops and transport—thus diverting attention from Gilly and me, flying together and some distance beneath them. . . .

A pilot landing at Valheureux at the end of the morning

reported that, although one of the balloons was not to be seen, the other was sailing, bloated with pride, at an altitude of some four thousand feet, to the south of the small town of Caudry. After a very light lunch we set out.

I mentioned the lightness of the lunch because we had to make sure of being alert on reaching the objective. The Germans on the other hand would, we hoped, be somnolent after beer and *blutwurst*, and therefore unlikely to notice us until too late to save their balloon. Wide awake and full of nothing but zeal we rushed across the lines at five thousand feet, Gilly slightly ahead, with me in the *Schweinhund* at his elbow and the protective flight high up so as not to alarm the enemy prematurely. For a moment the whole show appeared to me in bright colours, an exciting but not too dangerous adventure. Gilly waved an encouraging hand—I fancied I could hear him shout, 'Come on, chaps!' while the engine harmonised with the wires in that cheerful refrain of 'The Darktown Strutters' Ball. . . .' But not for long. When we were no more than half a mile beyond the German front lines, Archie opened up with a roar.

Perhaps, after all, the enemy had had a light lunch that day, at any rate they were not at all sleepy. By the time we reached Caudry several batteries of Archie were making good practice on us and 'flaming onions' were coming up in long strings of green fire. No chance of surprise. And, worse than that, not a sign of the balloon anywhere in the sky!

On most days an observation balloon would be plainly visible for many miles, but it's neutral colour—in autumn sunlight, with a faint mist in the air—sometimes camouflaged it so successfully that one might come within a thousand yards before remarking its ungainly shape. We hunted for it in all directions, high and low, into the sun, behind small clouds; until of a sudden I noticed Gilly banking his machine rapidly from side to side to attract my attention. I drew closer, saw him pointing down, and looked over the side of my cockpit. The balloon was on the ground—squatting ugly as a haggis, not a mile from Caudry. I glanced back at Gilly. . . . He was wagging his wings again. He was going down to attack.

Now given that you surprised the enemy there was no

reason why you shouldn't attack his balloons on the ground as easily as in the air. More easily in fact, for his guns had no time to come into action. That was how I got my first balloon: came upon him suddenly from over a ridge of hills, dived quickly, set him on fire, and away before Archie had fired a shot. But this was a very different matter. The enemy was warned of our coming and had a splendid view of our manœuvring; every machine-gunner must have been standing to, waiting to let fly.

That didn't stop Gilly. He had come out specially for that balloon and he wasn't going home without it. A moment after he had wagged his wings for the second time, he went over in a half-roll and shot downwards with a vertical dive like that of a stooping hawk. I remember the glimpse I had of his machine as it went down, and I remember, too, the thought which came to me: that in the face of the enemy's preparedness and of the barrage he was putting up, I would never have gone down alone. I was very thankful that he was the leader; it spared me any uncertainty as to what I had to do. Imitating his manœuvre of a half-roll, I followed him, stick well forward, engine at full throttle.

For the first few seconds of that dive I experienced a feeling resembling relief. The tension of waiting was over, we were going into action. And whatever trouble might await us below we had at least fooled Archie, leaving his shells to explode harmlessly a couple of thousand feet above us. . . . Gilly's speed increased tremendously—soon we must each of us have been doing two hundred and fifty*—and I had a hard time keeping up with him. I saw him whisk his head round once to see if I was following: imagined him calling, 'Hurry up, chaps!' and through my own mind there ran the answering yell, 'I'll be there to meet you in a taxi, honey. . . .' At fifteen hundred feet he opened fire.

I could see the long white smoke-streamers of Buckingham incendiary bullets tearing down into the balloon—and I could also see a string of 'flaming onions' coming up from close alongside. At about a thousand feet from the ground I too opened fire. For a few moments four machine-guns were firing at one balloon; its upper surface was becoming hazy, obscure; it was getting hot.

* The S.E.5's terminal velocity in a power dive was 275 m.p.h.

By now the earth was coming up pretty quickly. Intent on keeping my two guns upon the target, I missed seeing Gilly come out of his dive and I was so close to the ground myself when I pulled out that it seemed the earth must have swallowed him. No time to ponder the mystery of his disappearance. No time to think, no time to do anything except stop firing and flatten out of that intoxicating dive. Only just time to see the big bulge of black smoke coming from the balloon. The job was done. She was burning. I skimmed over the roof of a house. Made for home.

As if they had been waiting for this particular moment—as perhaps they had—the wakeful Germans now opened as hot an anti-aircraft fire as personally I have ever known. Effective shooting had not been possible hitherto owing to the great speed of our dive, but now that we were flying level again they had their chance and they took it. The amount of stuff they threw up in the next few seconds appalled me. And for once I couldn't find cover. Scattered houses and a line of trees barred the way back in such a manner that I could not get really low down to that contour-chasing flight which is safest of all in wartime. Holes began to appear in unpleasantly large numbers upon my wings, things jolted and rattled; I could see shell-splinters fly past, together with small splinters from the *Schweinhund*. And all at once there was a sort of explosion right in front of me, a puff of blue smoke, and a wave of petrol splashed into my face, half blinding me.

To this day I don't know whether it was an incendiary bullet, a 'flaming onion', or merely a bit of Archie, but a great hole opened up in my main tank, and that puff of smoke was thick and hot. . . .

Fire-terror seized me. I knocked back the throttle, groped unseeing for the switch, sideslipped violently to avoid the flames I expected. . . . The wind was cold on my cheek. I forced my eyes open. Petrol still whipped by, smarting intolerably; but there was no fire. I switched on again; nothing happened. No pressure, of course, and therefore no petrol. The voice that breathed o'er Eden bawled in my ear, 'Switch on to Gravity, you fool!' I fumbled with the petrol cock, the engine was slow in picking up. I was only a few feet from the ground, coming down very fast in an open field beyond the line of trees. No doubt of it, I was going to land

—in German territory. The engine coughed. I juggled frantically with the throttle-control.

And then the engine roared, jerked the machine forward, at length settled down to steady running. Air-speed rose quickly—eighty-five, ninety, a hundred. Heavy fire opened up ahead, machine-guns and rifles. I held the *Schweinhund* down, banked sharply round a clump of trees, dived over a low ridge, sped westward. The firing died away. . . .

XIV

It was later than usual when a motor-cycle and sidecar deposited me at the squadron. The orderly-clerk looked quite startled when I appeared in the doorway. But he seemed better pleased than on previous occasions.

'Fact is, sir,' he said, 'the returns have gone off to the wing. You're down as "missing, believed killed". I'm very pleased you're safe, sir, but—well, I'm glad I shan't have to do the returns all over again tonight.'

Apparently one of the protective flight pilots had seen me going down under heavy fire, and mixing my machine up with the flames and smoke of the balloon had reported me to have been '*carboneezay*', as Foxy would have said. Hence consternation in the mess, for the squadron, having had a good day, wanted to celebrate Gilly's destruction of the balloon, but felt a little doubtful about feasting until quite certain that I was good and dead. My sudden reappearance in the doorway of the pavilion, therefore, elicited a loud cheer, and after the usual shout of, 'Well, chaps, what happened to you?' the wine began to flow.

I was glad of that cheer because it showed that the squadron appreciated my luck. But later in the evening, just before the band began to play the squadron song, a second and louder cheer hailed the much more remarkable fact that I had remembered to bring back the watch.

XV

The war hurried on. And the time came for us to leave

that quiet orchard at Valheureux where in the intervals of long and perilous hours in the air, we had lived happily enough. Henceforth we moved restlessly forward from one aerodrome to another. For the long agony of the infantry in the trenches of the devastated areas was over at last, and although there was still much fighting to be done it would be mainly in the open and with the help of cavalry and tanks. Cambrai was in our hands, the Hindenburg Line a thing of the past. The troops were advancing over country hardly touched by war, to Le Cateau and Valenciennes.

The first aerodrome we settled at gave me something of a shock. The ground itself and the surrounding country had been badly knocked about in the past three years, but the features were still recognisable, which was more than could be said for most of the land from the Somme to the Scheldt. A German squadron had been stationed in the neighbourhood. They had lived and messed in a château nearby. Walking over their old aerodrome, I looked into the house. And fancied I could hear keen young voices talking of aerial fighting, of flying and of the performances of new machines; sharp, high-pitched voices, yet not wholly displeasing, although one of them spoke of *furchtbare Langeweile*. . . . Voices of the dead! It was the aerodrome close to which I had landed in my B.E.2c, and to which I had been taken a prisoner.

A few days later when I was driving with Gilly, helping to choose another more advanced aerodrome, we passed close to a squadron also about to move forward. A squadron engaged in artillery observation work. We drew up at the mess to ask for information about landing-grounds in the vicinity. I went into the mess-tent at the invitation of one of the officers, but that, it appeared, was as far as their hospitality went. Rather shamefacedly the officer accompanying me explained that the offering of drinks, meals, a packet of cigarettes, or indeed anything—except, I must suppose, first-aid to a wounded man—was against the rules of the mess. The coldness of our reception caused me to ask the number of this squadron. I was not surprised at the answer. But the officer who told me had never heard that his unit had for long been stationed on the western bank of the Lys. Nor did he know that the Starched Shirt had once commanded it. . . .

By the end of October we had advanced across the Scheldt to an aerodrome in the midst of that area, to the south-east of Cambrai, where but a little while previously German uniforms had daily drawn our fire, where desperate German machine-gunners had fought heroically. It seemed curious to be living and flying now from the district whence the enemy had faced so proudly and so long towards the Somme from the vaunted security of the Hindenburg Line. The French inhabitants, dazed by a liberation for which they had almost ceased to hope, stammered out tales of the years gone by, remembered the dates of our raids and fights, could tell us where pilots long dead had come down, where others had been captured. We discovered Larry Bowen's grave in a cemetery not far from the aerodrome he had raided; another, marked with a German cross, at the side of a quiet country road. . . . And at finding myself in this land over which the flame of war had passed like a forest fire, I had a strange feeling of disillusionment, almost amounting to sorrow at the enemy's departure. There came to me a sensation of emptiness, an inkling of futility—as if in grasping at what had seemed the bright substance of victory we had but stumbled a little farther into shadows.

It was then, too, that I chanced to read a sentence of Shaw's writing: about the joy of life—about 'being thoroughly worn out before you are thrown on the scrap heap'. The scrap heap? A pilot's life in France—allowing for death, injury or capture—averaged under six weeks. My time was more than up. How much longer would the luck hold? Towards the end it seemed to be a question of which would be finished first: myself or the war. . . .

There was much to be done yet. Bombing of troops and transport, machine-gunning of the retiring enemy, destruction of his strongpoints. And renewed fighting at high altitudes for the German aviators were busy again on our sector, struggling gamely to avert the now inevitable end. We banished gloomy thoughts and carried on somehow, seeking fights wherever they were to be found, anxious to raise the numbers of our successes for the greater glory of the squadron. But the canker of disillusionment gnawed at my heart. In Germany I had striven for liberty so as to return to France and flying. Now in France I was striving hard enough, but I scarcely knew for what. Final victory in the war was certain—but beyond that? I was becoming introspective, conscious of a deep change within myself since the days of the barge on the Lys, a change not wholly for the better. Eagerness, enthusiasm were still there, but blended with something very like despair.

XVI

The whirlwind continued to blow, but now the vortex shifted to higher altitudes. Although ground attacks were still almost daily events, my personal adventures were more concerned with aerial combats. It was a welcome change, but one which made matters none the easier, since owing to my aversion to fighting in formation I frequently became involved in fights from which—one S.E. versus many Fokkers —I was lucky to escape with a whole skin and a no more than badly battered *Schweinhund*. In the S.E.'s superior speed on the dive sometimes lay the only road to salvation.

A small share of victories did, however, come my way, in spite of unorthodox methods and inexperience, although I knew that I could never hope to achieve the virtuosity of the squadron's great pilots. It is on record that McCudden once brought down a German aeroplane with a single shot —luck if you like, but a sign that his methods were sound, his aim accurate. It is also on record that in the destruction of a solitary Fokker an S.E. pilot once expended five hundred and fifty rounds. I see no reason why I should reveal the identity of *that* pilot.

But I was no longer making a practice of fighting entirely alone. The American Johnny Speaks, a lanky Canadian known as Bloody Bob Caldwell (whose field-boots, however grimy his hands and face, were always speckless mirrors) and I now did much of our hunting together, whether on high patrols or near the ground. We were now almost the senior pilots in the squadron, the maintenance of its traditions was in our hands, so that closer co-operation in air-fighting brought a depth of friendship that had in it something of the 'Muske-teers'. And like those jolly warriors labelled Three for the sufficient reason that they were Four, so we had in Gilly a d'Artagnan who was both friend and leader.

I wish it were possible to give an ampler account of the doings of Johnny and Bob, but memory does not stretch that far. And though we compared notes of daily fighting and laid plans for future raids, when the four of us sat round the fire in the evenings it was not usually to talk of bloodshed. Moreover, it was an association which Chance did not permit to last very long.

XVII

One evening when I had just landed the *Schweinhund*, after she had had the good fortune to bring down a couple of Fokkers with no more damage than two holes through her radiator, I found Bob in the tent 'office', where I had gone to make out my report. His boots were immaculate as ever, but his face was long as a winter's night.

'Any luck?' he asked gloomily.

I told him the news, restraining my elation with difficulty.

'That's good!' he exclaimed grinning. 'Johnny got one too. The squadron record *is* going up.' His face grew sombre again. 'I'll have to hurry to catch up—it will soon be my last chance.'

'Why?' I asked in alarm. 'They aren't transferring you to another squadron, are they?'

'No, but it's all over now, bar the shouting.'

'What is? The squadron? They're sending us home to get the new machines?'

'No, not that either. We'll never get those new machines. It's the war—she's finished, done for. Fritz has thrown in the towel. Asking for peace. . . .'

I couldn't believe it. Nor could anyone else, not for days. It seemed impossible that it should be so. That great, strong German who had held us back for years—on his knees? True, since August he had been beaten everywhere, on all fronts, beaten so that he could not hope to attack again; but although he was now in full retreat he had not yet been pushed back as far as he had advanced. He still stood on French soil. And already he was crying for mercy? Couldn't stand up for the last round? No, it couldn't be true! It was

just the usual peace talk, a trick on the part of the enemy. . . .
Had we been in supreme command I think we should have
refused him the armistice he begged for.

XVIII

My last fight with a Fokker took place on November 3rd,
and my last aerial engagement—which is not to say that it
was when I fired my final shots—on November 5th. I suppose
that to celebrate the day I had hoped to arrange some specially
attractive display of pyrotechnics, but in that I was disappointed. For although, leading my patrol, I tried to force a fight
upon a formation of Fokkers they would have none of it, so
that at length I was compelled to demand satisfaction from
a humble, but by no means defenceless, kite-balloon sitting
over the eastern edge of Mormal Forest. And with defective
ammunition halting my attack it was the enemy who once
again provided the fireworks.

It did not occur to me at the time that this last engagement
was the counterpart of my very first. Just over three years
since, greatly daring, I had sauntered along in the Shorthorn
to vent my spite upon a German balloon near Loos. Then
the wind had whistled through piano wires like a gale amid
pine trees. Now I dived steeply in *Schweinhund III* and her
streamlined rigging screamed Wagnerian music. The result
was the same: the enemy hauled down his balloon.

Two days later something happened that was to mark my
memory for life, though the incident itself was commonplace
and small enough. It came about in this way. Leaving Johnny
to take over leadership of the Dawn Patrol, for the heavily
overcast skies were empty of enemy aircraft, I had gone down
to seek targets on the ground. Hunting around just before
sunrise I came presently to a more northerly sector of our
now rapidly changing front, where a small force of British
infantry, a battery of guns in support, could be seen moving
forward up the pock-marked western side of a long slope.
To the east, perhaps a hundred yards ahead of the most
advanced troops, the ground fell away over a low chalky cliff.
The German position, upon which our guns were dropping
occasional shells, must be below the cliff; circling round at a

distance I could tell almost exactly where it lay. I would have an easy target, diving over the cliff from the west, unseen by the enemy until I opened fire. There was to be an attack—I thought I would start it.

Skimming over the heads of our men I reached the edge of the cliff; and dived, engine roaring. With a thumb on the gun controls, I peered forward through the Aldis sight; and once more there came to me the sudden tightening of the nerves and of the heart that always returned whenever I was about to open fire, knowing that fire would be answered, that the next few seconds would be decisive one way or the other. I saw some half-dug trenches, a stunted tree, a patch of brushwood; a little way back from the foot of the cliff a number of gun positions, between them a road, a dead horse. And all at once I seemed to see, in a fleeting vision that compressed time into an instant, the whole melancholy prospect of our tardy victory.

And this is how I see it even now. A narrow country road, grey-white, stretches away to the east, cutting in two a monotonous brown plain. At broken intervals along the road, bordering untilled fields, rows of slender poplars stand straight and motionless. There is no wind; in the damp stillness of the autumn air I can see leaves falling vertically. Near at hand a ruined farmhouse stares through a pair of shattered windows like one whose eyes have not been closed in death: beside it a barn smothered in smoke burns steadily. From local flooding have come dark pools of stagnant water in the farmyard, at the side of the road, in the fields. Recent shell-holes grouped unevenly have a sickly yellowish look as though the land has been stricken by some repulsive disease. Through their midst the wet, faintly gleaming road leads on, growing ever narrower to vanish at last into the November fog as though into the heart of infinity—the long hard road back into Belgium where, for us, the war had started. In the distance beyond the farmhouse a handful of men in faded grey uniforms push, drag, hurry beside a hand-cart heavily laden. Of the might of a great nation, of its arrogance and military pomp, they are the sole remnants. At their thoughts as they return, perhaps not empty-handed but certainly defeated, to the fatherland whence they marched so proudly, I can but guess. Yet in their manner of striding on there seems

to be a purpose, a common resolve urging them to follow
the road to its mysterious end.

So much I saw in a matter of seconds as my aeroplane
rushed towards this desolate land—perhaps the more desolate for not being utterly devastated. But before I had time
to absorb it all, I received another and more disconcerting
impression. As I dived over the edge of the cliff and looked
down into the shallow trenches I saw that they were empty.
Bits and pieces of equipment, barbed wire, a smashed limber,
corrugated iron from a temporary shelter—the refuse of war
—lay scattered; but not an armed man was to be seen. In
uncompleted gun-pits three or four howitzers remained,
rendered useless no doubt; but the attendant gunners had
gone. The position was deserted. And then, through the
narrow circle of the Aldis sight, I saw him—the only enemy
soldier left in the vicinity of this hastily abandoned strong-
point.

That one unexpected glimpse as I flattened out of the dive
less than fifty feet from the ground will stay in my mind for
ever. In the course of the war I had seen, like everyone else,
dead men in every sickening phase of putrescence; had heard
the wounded cry out; had watched, without power to help,
men burning to death or falling from the sky; I was inured
to horror. Yet this, seen at the very moment when in un-
thinking anger I was about to fire both guns at a supposedly
numerous enemy, filled me with sudden dismay. I shall see
that German soldier always. He is for me the Beginning and
the End of war. He lies across the road by which his friends
have marched in triumph or in sorrow first in one direction,
now in the other, but always, I think, with the horizon
obscured by mist. He is young, fair-haired—his steel helmet
has fallen off; from the length of his limbs he must have been
tall. He lies on his back mortally wounded. Something—
perhaps a steel splinter, for the earth close by is newly
shell-torn—has severed his right arm near the shoulder and
laid bare his breast so that I can almost see the ribs through
the dreadful red tatters of flesh. His mouth hangs open; he
gasps for the breath that will but prolong his suffering. He
is alone, forsaken. As I thunder over his head he draws up
a leg convulsively, the boot scraping a little trench in the
mud beneath which he will presently rest. He lies between

the armies; just one dying youth, nothing in the war; uncared
for, unnoticed. But not unnoticeable, for he bars the road.
They will have to move him before they pass, whoever they
are. Behind the slope above the cliff our own young men are
advancing. To attack what? After all the years of hope, of
failure, of stubborn courage, of lives thrown away like burnt
match-sticks, leaving a million dead behind them they are
to strike at—nothing. Their wrath, like mine, will spend
itself in the air. And they will only march to victory across
the body of dead Youth. . . .

As I flew on eastward above the muddy road, I overtook
the half-dozen German soldiers struggling along with their
hand-cart. Before I reached them I saw one unsling his
rifle and throw it up to his shoulder. Standing firm, legs
apart and aiming well ahead of my machine, he looked like
a statue of exasperated humanity firing its small thunder at
the mute, uncomprehending heavens. One of his shots
cracked past, close to my head. I did not reply. It was no
longer worth while.

That same evening I left for England. My turn for leave
had come. It was about time. Over nine weeks had passed
since my return to the front. The luck could not have held
much longer. and this was the leave that had been due in
December, 1915.

XIX

It would have been easy to have stayed on in England
after my leave was up, but France drew me back irresistibly.
Even now many of us were not sure that the war was over,
it still seemed incredible that Germany should have collapsed
so suddenly and completely. We thought it more than likely
that back on his own soil, rested, reorganised, strengthened,
the enemy would make a stand, defy us to come farther.
The Armistice would be denounced; there would be a flare
up of fighting from the embers of war; we should have to
force our way into the Rhineland, and final victory would
still await the coming of spring. After the noisy celebrations
in London we trooped back.

Gilly had told me in London that he was to be invalided

home; I was to be in command of the squadron, of *the* squadron—that alone was sufficient reason for rejoining. We had changed aerodromes once more, to quarters not far from Caudry—and near the very spot to which I had once followed Gilly in that wild dive upon a balloon. The place was silent now, too silent. All through the old war areas, from Albert to St Quentin, from Arras to Cambrai and on to Le Cateau, the land was desolate, deserted, for the armies had already moved on, the French civilians not yet returned. Sometimes at the end of a misty autumn afternoon the silence would become appalling—like the grave, like being buried alive. Amid the wreckage of a war that was over, with the litter of equipment, the shell-holes, the scattered crosses all about one, there seemed to be more than just silence in the air. It was as though from each day of the Four Years some ghostly event were rising to call to us, to remind us of the dead past; as though the dead themselves were calling us back. . . . We made a great deal of noise in the mess to drown such mournful sounds, and spent as much time as possible in the air.

Schweinhund III had survived the war, although the wind hummed through her wires more gently now. Without Archie's alarming cough or the sharp crackle of machine-gun bullets there was no need for them to sing too loud a song. But I made them scream again when the troops moved forward; dived at abandoned German aerodromes, hedge-hopped over liberated Belgium, overtook joyfully waving infantry advancing with the Army of the Rhine.

The Rhine! I flew down it, dived to the water's edge at Cologne, zoomed over the Cathedral and the railway station where, a prisoner, I had spent many cold and depressing hours; followed the railway to Aachen, circled the town, flew to the Dutch frontier, stared down. . . . There I had crossed to freedom, along that white thread of a road beside that wood. Now I roared over the spot in an S.E.5, its nose painted bright red, with *Schweinhund* in large white letters to annoy the enemy. A triumphant return! But somehow, even as I looked down at that little corner of the earth which I had been at such pains to reach, an inexplicable fit of melancholy seized me. Disenchantment had made rapid strides. The Dutch frontier, the war, even flying seemed to have lost their meaning. Things which for years had mattered more than life itself were no longer of any great importance—to me or to anyone else.

Banking the *Schweinhund* steeply I turned away and, without looking back, laid a straight course for Brussels, wine and women. . . .

'Brussels by Christmas'—no difficulty about that any more! But we did not go there then; we preferred to spend Christmas in the squadron, having our own ideas of how to celebrate. And considering the miserable state of things —half peace, half war—we made quite a good show of it. Turkeys? No, they were not to be found. With their antiquated knowledge of aerodynamics they must have succumbed to Progress in northern France at about the same time as the Shorthorn. But geese there were, and we purchased them in quantity for the men as well as for the pilots.

I fancy the men had a reasonably good Christmas that year. In addition to the geese, valuable supplies were secretly obtained, a barrel of beer was set up in the mess-room, an extra ration of rum issued. And the only incident worthy of the name was when an exasperated engine-fitter, armed with an axe, chased the disciplinary sergeant-major round the aerodrome in the cold dawn of Boxing Day. . . . But such high spirits were natural to the men of that squadron. Each man an expert in his own line, they had worked with a will. Upon their careful tuning of engines, their skilful adjustment of rigging wires, their accurate sighting of machine-guns, many lives had long depended. The squadron's successes are theirs to share with the boldest of those pilots whose names still head the Honours board. The magic brilliance of those letters, 'V.C.', twice repeated, shines on them as well; they helped to carve them.

XX

Johnny, Bob and I flew to Brussels to hail the New Year. It was our last celebration. Early in January we were informed officially that the squadron was not going up to the Rhine as we had hoped it would, and that demobilisation would commence at once.

For a few weeks more we carried on working, flying, practising formations and firing our guns at targets hoping against hope that something might yet occur to keep us together; and then slowly but with gathering speed the squadron began to dwindle like a community stricken by the plague. The men went first and the officers from overseas. Each morning in the office I would find a fresh list of those to whom release had come much as the Summons came for Mr Valiant-for-Truth, but in place of the Pitcher broken at the Fountain were the tokens of equipment, of tools, of flying-kit returned to store. The orchestra played 'The Darktown Strutters' Ball' for the last time and were dispersed. Skilled mechanics vanished one by one, men who had been with the squadron from the start, ever since the day when, proud of its new S.E.s, it had come to France to put fear into a strong and determined enemy. Pilots flew for the last time and packed up their kits; the mess grew smaller. Young Canadians, South Africans, Americans whom we had just had time to understand and to like disappeared from our lives forever. The senior N.C.O.s, without whom the squadron could not function, shook hands and entrained—rather regretfully, I thought—for demobilisation camps in England. The silence became so much the heavier that at length we were too few to lift it.

Then the final blow fell. In February our machines, our beloved S.E.s which we had come to regard as our personal property to endow with all the affection men give to ships, were taken away from us—flown down to a depot to be, in the official phrase, 'reduced to produce', destroyed.

Before she left I cut from the side of *Schweinhund III* the three-ply panel bearing her name. I took it home with me, a vain reminder of the days of her greatness. . . .

In the end Bob Caldwell went on leave to England and did not return. He wrote me from the ship in which he sailed to Canada, but I never saw him again. He went in for experimental parachute work in his own country. During an exhibition flight to prove the safety of parachutes he jumped from an aeroplane. The parachute failed to open.

After his departure, Johnny Speaks, Bill the acting-adjutant and I were the only ones left in the mess to dine in state—three where there had been twenty-three!—beneath that

scroll of honour which in a small measure we had helped
to lengthen. . . .

A few transport drivers still remained, and the orderly-
room clerk whom I had so distressed by my late returns
from patrols and ground-*strafes* sat faithfully by his records
in the deserted office.

Three motor-bicycles, once furiously ridden by despatch
riders with urgent news, had been retained until the end, and
on these we toured the neighbourhood, visiting the graves
of those who had been killed from the squadron, taking a
last look at the places above which we had fought. In
Cambrai I found the gateway where I had caught a company
of sheltering Germans; bullet holes and scratches from my
machine-gun fire showed up plainly—a mark that would
not soon be erased.

One morning, when the snow lay thick upon the old
battlefields and grey clouds hung low in a windless sky, I
said goodbye to Johnny. A string of lorries waited outside
the mess; he was taking the remains of the squadron to the
base depot and so back to England.

'Hope to see you in London in a few days,' he said. 'I
shan't be sailing for America for a long time yet.'

'What are you going to do when you're demobilised?'

'Try to get a flying job somewhere, I suppose. It's about
the only thing worth doing right now. You're staying on in
the Air Force, aren't you?'

I nodded.

'Yes, for what it's worth—after all this.'

Johnny looked slowly over the whitened hills towards the
village where his friend Larry now slept beneath the cross
of his own propeller.

'Funny, after a rotten war like this, how hard it is to leave.'
He sighed. And then smiled quickly to hide his feelings.
'War's all wrong, I guess, but—ah well, them *was* the happy
days, them was! Goodbye, G.-M.'

The lorries rumbled away down the long straight road to
Cambrai. I watched them go, I, the only one left of all the
men in that once powerful squadron; for the acting-adjutant
had been posted to England with the records, the last men
had travelled down to the base, even the orderly-room clerk
had gone. And with the final break-up of the squadron every-

thing that had given zest to life seemed to have gone too. The deep rumble of the lorries died away, and in the wintry silence which then fell, the only sound I could hear was the faint humming of telegraph wires—feeble echo of past endeavour.

Index

Library of Congress Cataloging-in-Publication Data

Grinnell-Milne, Duncan William.
Wind in the wires / Duncan Grinnell-Milne.
p. cm. — (Wings of war)
Originally published: London : Jarrolds, 1971.
Includes index.
ISBN 0-8094-9629-1 (trade). — ISBN 0-8094-9630-5 (library)
1. Grinnell-Milne, Duncan William.
2. World War, 1914-1918—Aerial operations, British.
3. World War, 1914-1918—Personal narratives, British.
4. Air pilots, Military—Great Britain—Biography.
I. Series.
D602.G73 1992   940.54'4941—dc20   92-6550 CIP

Published by arrangement with Harold Ober Associates.

Cover photograph © Carl Purcell
Endpapers photograph © Rene Sheret/After Image